Offences Against Children

Socio-legal Perspectives

Offences Against Children

Socio-legal Perspectives

K. Kumar and Punam Rani

Regency Publications
New Delhi 110 008

ISBN 81-86030-31-X

Published by Regency Publications, 20/36-G, Old Market, West Patel Nagar, New Delhi 110 008 and printed at Radiant Printers, New Delhi, Phones: 571 3968, 578 3571.

FOREWORD

I have a great pleasure in writing a foreword to the book titled "*Offences against Children—Sociolegal Perspectives*" authored by Shri K. Kumar, Advocate, and Member, Supreme Court Bar Association and his daughter Punam Rani of National Institute of Social Defence, Ministry of Welfare, Government of India, New Delhi.

The authors have tried to focus the attention of the community towards the importance of children as national asset and the sad plight to which they are put in, in the present scenario presumably on account of various social factors. The whole work has been compiled in eleven chapters, each dealing with specific subject. The first chapter is Prelude, which is an introductory chapter and the last chapter is Postscript included by way of conclusion. The second chapter pertains to the laws relating to children. The main theme has been dealt with in 111 pages systematized into eight chapters each dealing with a particular aspect. At the end is appended the full text of the "*Convention on the Rights of Child*" as adopted by the United Nations General Assembly on November 20, 1989. A reading of this Convention gives an insight into the goal required to be achieved, to what extent it has been achieved and what yet remains to be achieved. The chapters are replete with number of instances reinforced with legal provisions and legal pronouncements, and the same makes the book very informative and interesting.

The significance of the book is that it meets the critical need for a text which will serve as an essential literature required for acquiring a thought-provoking view-points on the subject. The book, therefore, is a welcome addition to the already existing literature and will prove useful in fields of law and social sciences.

I trust this book will inspire contemplation in readers and provoke further debates and discussions on the subject and it is hoped that it will find a suitable place in every library dealing with law and social sciences.

New Delhi
20th July, 1996

K.B. SINHA
Former Judge, Patna High Court

PREFACE

Children constitute nearly 38 perc ent of the country's population and have been declared as national assets by the Apex Court in *Sheela Barse & Another* v. *Union of India, AIR 1986 SC 1873*. They are innocent and helpless guys and need proper care and nourishment during the growing years so that they become useful members of the society. Are children receiving the attention and care which they deserve? The answer in respect of a majority of children could be 'probably no'. Rather they are the objects of neglect and pity on account of various factors including poverty, unchecked population growth and lack of education and enlightenment of the parents.

The authors have made an attempt to focus the attention of the community, through the pages of this book, towards the sad plight of the children during their early and growing years. It is aimed at providing a food for thought on this issue which is currently very important.

Our thanks are due to Hon'ble Justice (Retd.) K.B. Sinha, former Judge of the High Court of Judicature at Patna, at present a Senior Counsel of the Supreme Court India. He spared his valuable time in going through the chapters of the book, made valuable suggestions and wrote an inspiring foreword.

The authors are greatly inspired by the work of UNICEF, which during 50 years of its existence had made significant contribution to the cause of children on global level. The organisation has issued a literature *"Convention on the Rights of Child"* which provides an insight into the rights of a child and what they deserve and how much attention has been paid by the various functionaries in the country and Indian society. The same has been appended at the end of this book, for a ready reference. The authors owe their gratefulness to the UNICEF. The authors are further obliged to the local newspapers for various news items that enlightened the authors as regards the childrens' problems in the present scenario.

The authors are indebted to some of the luminaries and scholars in the field of social sciences. Particular mention is made of Dr. S.K. Bhattacharya a colleague of the author, K. Kumar for his valuable advice and suggestions from time to time. The authors would like to thank the team of M/s Regency Publications for bringing out this book in a nice manner in a record time.

Any critical and constructive criticism from the readers shall be gratefully acknowledged.

Supreme Court of India
Bhagwan Das Road
New Delhi 110 001

KAUSHALENDRA KUMAR

National Institute of Social
Defence, (Ministry of Welfare)
Government of India
New Delhi 110 066

PUNAM RANI

CONTENTS

Chapter I

PRELUDE

1.01 Introduction

A child is a national asset.[1] A child, who is born, is thrust into an unfamiliar world and is left at the mercy of adults. A responsive and sensible adult is loving and caring but the irresponsibility and the insensitivity of an adult results in commission of various offences, impliedly and expressly. Giving birth to a child without having proper means and his neglect amounts to implied offence and brutalities, molestations, abuse etc. are express crimes.

Usually the infantile dependence touches the responsive chords of adults, who take delight in caring for the child.[2] It is the need of the hour that the agencies like sensible parents at home, dutiful teachers in school, a good and responsible government, honest public servants and responsible politicians having the heart and will to do good to the people, should take up the cause of the children and implement all that is needed for their proper growth and development. In that event, the innocent, independent and helpless guys, the national asset, would be fully prepared to face all that is needed in life and march ahead with time.

1. 02 Problem Areas in the Present Scenario

The following are the problem areas in the present world on a global level.[3]

1. One third of the developing world's children suffer from protein-energy malnutrition.

2. An estimated 2,50,000 children lose their eye-sight annually for lack of vitamin A.
3. On account of the deficiency in iodine, an estimated 50 million children are victims of impaired development.
4. As a sequel to the decline in breast-feeding, millions of infants are exposed to illness, poor growth and early death.
5. A major nutritional problem is the lack of iodine in food. In addition to affecting the normal development of the children numbering nearly 50 million, an estimated 1,00,000 infants are born every year as cretins. It has been ascertained that 1.6 billion people are at risk with consequences ranging from goitre to reduced mental and physical performance.
6. The greatest threats to the health of children in the developing world are measles, diarrhoea and pneumonia. On account of the poor nutrition, these three diseases kill approximately 7 million children per year and leave millions malnourished. Diarrheal disease alone kills almost 3 million children every year. A million are killed every year by measles and over 3 millions by pneumonia.
7. Tetanus kills an estimated 6,00,000 new-borns and 50,000 children lose their mothers during birth every year.
8. Today there are several millions of children, in economically advanced nations, whose quality of life would have to be judged poorer than that of many children in the developing world.
9. A significant number of children in the rich world live in poverty—approximately 5, 10 and 20 per cent in Western Europe, Australia, Canada and the U.K. and in the United States of America respectively.
10. Murder of and suicide by young people have been steadily increasing in the industrialized countries.
11. An estimated 10 to 15 per cent of children in industralized nations are victims of child-abuse. This estimate is on the basis of reported cases but it is difficult to make correct assessment on account of many cases going unreported and/or undetected.
12. In the family environment, the lives of many children are emptying of close relations as family size falls, divorce rate rises and parents spend more time outside the home.

13. In the economic environment, children are in the front line of the difficult transitions being made.
14. In the physical environment, children are the most vulnerable to adult mistakes.

1.03 Efforts by 'WHO' and 'UNICEF'

In 1994, the executive heads of WHO (World Health Organisation) and UNICEF (United Nations Children's Fund) as the orginasations for monitoring and improving the well-being of children in all nations brought out relevant data on child survival; health, nutrition, education, family planning and progress in respect of women. These two organizations have written to all Heads of State with an appeal for leadership in achieving ten priority social goals by the end of 1995. In that letter, it has been urged upon that the achievements of the 1995 goals would serve as a foundation for achieving the longer-term targets already agreed to, for the year 2000. The end-of-century goals and the expected achievements are summarized as under:[4]

The 10 goals of 1995

(1) The raising of immunization coverage to at least 80 per cent.
(2) The elimination of neo-natal tetanus.
(3) Measures for reduction in measle deaths and cases.
(4) The eradication of polio.
(5) The achievement of 80 per cent ORT (Oral Rehydration Therapy).
(6) Support for breast-feeding through the 'baby-friendly' hospitals initiative and the ending of free and low-cost distribution of breast-milk substitutes.
(7) The elimination of vitamin A deficiency.
(8) The universal iodization of salt.
(9) The virtual elimination of guinea-worm disease.
(10) The universal ratification of the Convention on the Rights of the Child.

Achievement by the end-of-century goals

(1) One-third reduction in under-five death rates.
(2) Reduction of maternal mortality death by half.
(3) Reduction in severe and moderate mal-nutrition among the

world's under-five children by half. The elimination of micro-nutrient disorders, support for breast-feeding by all hospitals and maternity units and a reduction in the incidence of low birth weight to less than 10 per cent.

(4) Achievement and maintenance of at least 90 per cent immunization coverage for infants and universal tetanus immunization for women in the child-bearing years, the eradication of polio, the elimination of neonatal tetanus, a 90 per cent reduction in measles cases and a 95 per cent reduction in measles deaths (compared to levels before immunization).
(5) Achievement of 80 per cent ORT (Oral Rehydration Therapy) use and bringing down by 50 per cent, child deaths caused by diarrhoea.
(6) A reduction by 30 per cent (that is: nearly one-third) in child deaths from acute respiratory infections.
(7) Basic education for all children and completion of primary education by at least 80 per cent, both boys and girls.
(8) Safe drinking water and sanitation for all families.
(9) Acceptance and observance, in all countries, of the Convention on the Rights of the Child.
(10) Family planning education and services to be made available to all.

1.04 Rights of Child

In 1989, the U.N. General Assembly adopted the Convention on the Rights of Child. On 2nd September 1990, the Convention entered into force as International Law, within a year, more than 90 countries had ratified and by the end of September 1995, the total was 179. No Human Rights Convention had ever attained such widespread ratification.

The Government of India acceded to the Convention on the 11th December 1992.

The Convention established Social and Economic Rights—right to survival, early development, education, health care and social welfare support. It also covers civil and political rights. These include the right of a child to a name and nationality, freedom of expression and participation in decision affecting his or her wellbeing.

The key underlying advance was the recognition of the child as a complete individual. The Convention establishes that a child has an identity distinct from parents or nurturers and that the community has a duty to protect that identity and enable the child to express it in matters such as guardianship or custody. In these areas, the consideration should be the best interest of the child (see Appendix I at the end of this book).

REFERENCES

1. *Sheela Barse and another* v. *U.O.I. & others, AIR 1986 SC 1973.*
2. Mallika Akbar, "Abuse—a vicious circle," *The Sunday Times (Delhi Edition) Nov. 19, 1995*
3. See Arts. 23, 24 of the Convention on the Rights of Child (Appendix I).
4. Sources—Summary, The State of the World's Children 1996. UNICEF, p. 11, Col. 2.

Chapter II

LAWS APPLICABLE TO CHILDREN

2.01 Definition of Child

The expression *'child'* has been defined variously under various Acts. Child means a person who has not completed the age of 16 years.[1] A *minor* is one who has completed the age of 16 years but has not completed the age of 18 years.[2] A person who has completed the age of 18 years is a *major*.[3] The Children Act, 1960[4] defines child as meaning a boy who has not attained the age of 16 years and a girl who has not attained the age of 18 years. The Juvenile Justice Act, 1986[5] has substituted the word *'Juvenile'* in the definition clause for *'child'*. The Child Labour (Prohibition and Regulation) Act, 1986 defines child as a person who has not completed his 14 years.[6] The Factories Act [7] defines child as one who has not completed his 15th year of age. According to the *'Convention on the Rights of Child'* [8] which was adopted by the General Assembly of the United Nations on 20th November 1989 and acceded by the Government of India on 11th December 1992, every human being below the age of 18 years is included in the category of child unless under the law applicable to the child, majority is attained earlier.

The childhood period is above the age of 6 years and below the age of 18 years, that is; in the period that lies between infancy and puberty. The term means a person under the age of 14 years and when used in reference to a child sent to a Certified School applies to that child during the period of detention, notwithstanding that child attains the age of 14 years before the expiration of that period. With reference to non-power Factories Act and Shops and Commercial Establishment Act, the term *'child'* means a person who has not completed 14 years.[9]

2.02 Right of Birth and Survival

Every child in the mother's womb has the right to be born and survive as a general rule unless there are certain special circumstances against it. Sections 312 to 318 of the IPC[10] provides punishments for voluntarily causing abortion thus destroying it in embryonic stage and preventing its birth. Section 312 prescribes punishments extending to 7 years imprisonment and fine for causing miscarriage, unless the same has taken place in good faith. Section 313 provides a sentence of imprisonment extending to 10 years or to life and also with fine when the miscarriage has been caused without woman's consent. Where death is caused in consequence of an act with intent to cause miscarriage, the person, who has done it, shall be punished with imprisonment of either description for a term which may extend to ten years and also to fine and if the act in question has taken place without the consent of the woman, the punishment may extend to life imprisonment in accordance with the provision of Section 314. Where miscarriage is caused with intent to prevent child being born or to cause it to die after birth, the offence falls within the scope of Section 315 IPC and the punishment may extend to imprisonment of either description for a term which may be ten years or with fine or with both unless the act has been done in good faith for saving the life of the mother. Whoever causes death of a quick unborn child by an act amounting to culpable homicide and does, by such act, cause the death of a quick unborn child makes himself liable for punishment with imprisonment of either description which may extend to ten years and also to fine under the provision of Section 316 IPC. Where the incident of birth is concealed by secret disposal of the dead body of a child, the punishment prescribed under Section 318 of the Code is two years of imprisonment with fine, or the punishment may be fine only.

Section 317 of IPC prescribes punishment for exposure and abandonment of child under 12 years of age by parent or person having care of it, which may extend to seven years of imprisonment or with fine or with both.

2.03 Provision of Medical Termination of Pregnancy Act

With the expansion of health services, when more people come to avail of the medical facilities in hospitals, doctors have come across cases of gravely ill or dying pregnant women whose pregnant uterus were tampered with in order to cause miscarriage of pregnancy, resulting in untold hardships to the woman. There is, thus, untold hardship coupled with unavoidable wastage of mother's health, strength and at times, loss of life. 'The Medical Termination of Pregnancy Act' was enacted in the year 1972 in order to liberalise certain existing provisions relating to pregnancy which could be terminated on the following three grounds:[11]

(1) *As a health measure*—When there is danger to the life or risk to the physical or mental health of the woman;

(2) *On humanitarian ground*—Such as when pregnancy arises in consequence of a sex crime like rape or sexual intercourse with a lunatic woman etc., and

(3) *Eugenic grounds*—Where there is substantial risk that the child, if born, would suffer from deformities and diseases.

The termination of pregnancy could be done in accordance with Sections 3, 4 and 5 of the M.R.P. Act, 1971[12] Section 3(2)(a) provides that a medical practitioner can terminate a pregnancy where the length of the pregnancy does not exceed 12 weeks. The time limit of 12 weeks has been fixed because life of the child in the womb starts after 12 weeks.

In order to judge the deformity of the child in the mother's womb, resort has to be taken of the knowledge of 'GENETIC TECHNOLOGY'. The genetic techniques, in addition to the determination of the deformities and no deformity, makes it possible to determine the sex of the child. The availability of this technique together with the provision of Medical Termination of Pregnancy Act, has led to the misuse of the two in causing abortion of the female fetus, in effect there is substantial lowering of female population.

2.04 Right to Free and Compulsory Education

Article 45 of the Constitution of India is a 'Directive Principle of State Policy' which envisages to provide, within a period of ten years from the commencement of the Constitution, free and compulsory education for all children until they complete the age of 14 years (see chapter on Schooling a Child for details).

2.05 Right against Exploitation

Right against exploitation is a fundamental right and these have been spelt out in the Constitution of India through Articles 23 and 24 in the following words:

Art. 23. Prohibition of traffic in human beings and forced labour.

(1) Traffic in human beings and *begar* and other similar forced labour are prohibited and any contravention of this provision shall be an offence punishable in accordance with law.

(2) Nothing in this Article shall prevent the State from imposing compulsory service for public purposes, and in imposing such service, the State shall not make any discrimination on grounds only of religion, race, caste or class or any one of them.

Art 24. Prohibition of employment of children in factories, etc.

No child below the age of fourteen years shall be employed to work in any factory or mine or engaged in any other hazardous employment.

2.06 Right to Health and Development in a Healthy Manner

The State is required to follow certain principles of policy towards securing among others, the following:[13]

(i) that the health and strength of workers, men and women, and the tender age of children are not abused and that citizens are not forced by economic necessity to enter avocations unsuited to their age or strength;

(ii) that children are given opportunities and facilities to develop in a healthy manner and in conditions of freedom and dignity and that childhood and youth are protected against exploitation and against moral and material abandonment.

2.07 Raising of the Level of Health and Nutrition

It is the duty of the state to raise the level of nutrition and the standard of living and to improve public health of its people as spelt out in the following words in Art. 47 of the Constitution of India:

> "The State shall regard the raising of the level of nutrition and the standard of living of its people and the improvement of public health as among its primary duties and, in particular, the state shall endeavour to bring about prohibition of the consumption except for medicinal purposes of intoxicating drinks and of drugs which are injurious to health."

2.08 Presumption of Legitimacy

Section 112 of the Evidence Act provides that birth of child during continuance of a valid marriage is a conclusive proof of legitimacy.[14] Section 112 lays down that if a person was born during the continuance of a valid marriage between his mother and any man within 280 days after its dissolution and the mother remained unmarried, it shall be taken as conclusive proof that he is the legitimate son of that man, unless it can be shown that the parties to the marriage had no access to each other at any time when he could have been begotten. This rule of law has always made the Courts of law inclined towards upholding the legitimacy of a child unless the facts are so compulsive and clinching as to necessarily warrant a finding that the child could not at all have been begotten to the father and as such a legitimation of the child would result in rank injustice to father. Courts have desisted from rendering a verdict in haste on the basis of slender materials that will have the effect of branding a child as a bastard and its mother an unchaste woman.[15] The special protection given by law to the status of legitimacy of a child has a social implication. No amount of proof that the mother committed adultery with any number of men can have adverse effect on the legitimacy of a child if she had access to her husband during the period when the child could have been conceived. The evidence of non-access for that purpose must be very strong, distinct, satisfactory and conclusive. These rigours are justified by considerations of public policy as the stigma of illegitimacy is considered to be very severe.[16]

2.09 Right to Maintenance

Section 125 of the Code of Criminal Procedure, 1973 (2 of 1974),[17] empowers a Magistrate of the First Class to order a person having sufficient means to make a monthly allowance limited to five hundred rupees to his wife, unable to maintain herself, or his legitimate or illegitimate child, minor or a sufferer of mental or physical infirmity or a victim of some injury.

NOTES

Vide Bill No. XXXV of 1994, Cr.P.C. (Amendment) Bill, Sec. 17, the word 'five hundred' has been substituted by 'one thousand five hundred.'

The right of a child, both legitimate and illegitimate, to get maintenance, is an independent right.[18] The child's right to maintenance is not affected by the provisions of the Muslim (Protection of Divorce) Act.[19]

2.10 Right to Property

According to Section 8 of the Hindu Succession Act (no. 30 of 1956) read with Schedule I, and Section 37 of the Indian Succession Act (no. 36 of 1925), children are entitled to a right in the property of his or her father or grand father/great grand father. Section 20 of the Hindu Succession Act, 1956,[20] provides right for the child in womb to inherit to the intestate after being born alive.

2.11 Minor's Estate under Islamic Law[21]

In Section 359 only the father, an executor appointed by father's will, father's father and the executor appointed by the will of the father's father are the legal guardians of property of a minor. No other relation is entitled to be the guardian of the property of a minor as of right, not even the mother, brother or uncle, but the father or the paternal grand father of the minor may appoint the mother, brother or uncle or any other person as his executor or executrix of his will in which they become legal guardians and have all the power of the legal guardian as defined in Section 362 and Section 366 of the above principles.

As per Section 362, the legal guardian of the property of a minor has no power to sell the immovable property of the minor except in the cases:

(1) where he can obtain double its value;
(2) where the minor has no other property and the sale is necessary for his maintenance;
(3) where there are debts of the deceased and no other means of paying them;
(4) where there are legacies to be paid and there are no other means of paying them;
(5) where the expenses exceeded the income of the property;
(6) where the property is falling into decay; and
(7) when the property has been usurp and the guardian has reason to fear that there is no chance of fair restitution.

In the absence of such guardians, property guardian appointed by the Court would be competent to alienate property of the minor with the permission of the Court.

> "When a sale is to be made on behalf of a minor, the necessary ingredients are that the sale must be for the benefit of the Estate of the minor and, therefore, the competent person entitled to alienate the minor's property would be either the natural guardian or the property guardian appointed by the Court."

2.12 Competency of Child as a Witness

A child is a competent witness to testify like all other witnesses if he has the capacity to understand the questions put to him and he offers a rational answer, in accordance with Section 118 of the Indian Evidence Act.[22]

2.13 Conclusion

In applying laws to the children, the paramount importance is the welfare of the child concerned.

REFERENCES

1. Section 2 (aa) of Immoral Traffic (Prevention) Act, 1956 as amended by Act no. 44 of 1986.
2. Section 2(cb)—*ibid.*
3. Section 2(ca)—*ibid.*
4. Section 2(e) of the Children Act, 1969.
5. Section 2(h) of the Juvenile Justice Act, 1986. In this definition the expression 'child' has been substituted by the word 'juvenile'. Both the terms, therefore, connote the same sense.
6. Vide Section 2(II) of the Child Labour (Prohibition and Regulation) Act, 1986.
7. Vide Section 2(c) of the Factories Act.
8. Vide Article 1 of the Convention.
9. Kumar, K. "R.I. Gupta's Medico-Legal Aspects of Sexual offence." 3rd Edition (1991), Eastern Book Company, 34 Lalbagh, Lucknow 226001.
10. Sections 312—318 I.P.C. Read as under:

Of the causing of miscarriage, of injuries to unborn children, of the exposure of infants, and of the concealment of births

312. *Causing miscarriage:* Whoever voluntarily causes a woman with child to miscarry, shall, if such miscarriage be not caused in good faith for the purpose of saving the life of the woman, be punished with imprisonment of either description for a term which may extend to three years, or with fine, or with both; and, if the woman be quick with child, shall be punished with imprisonment of either description for a term which may extend to seven years, and shall also be liable to fine.

Explanation: A woman who causes herself to miscarry, is within the meaning of this Section.

313. *Causing miscarriage without woman's consent:* Whoever commits the offence defined in the last preceding Section without the consent of the woman, whether the woman is quick with child or not, shall be punished with imprisonment for life, or with imprisonment of either description for a term which may extend to ten years, and shall also be liable to fine.

314. *Death caused by act done with intent to cause miscarriage:* Whoever, with intent to cause the miscarriage of a woman with child, does any act which causes the death of such woman, shall be punished with imprisonment of either description for a term which may extend to ten years, and shall also be liable to fine;

[if act done without woman's consent] and if the act is done without the consent of the women, shall be punished either with imprisonment for life, or with the punishment above mentioned.

Explanation: It is not essential to this offence that the offender should know that the act is likely to cause death.

315. *Act done with intent to prevent child being born alive or to cause it to die after birth:* Whoever before the birth of any child does any act with the intention of thereby preventing the child from being born alive or causing it to die after its birth, and does by such act prevent that child from being born alive, or causes it to die after its birth, shall, if such act be not caused in good faith for the purpose of saving the life of the

mother, be punished with imprisonment of either description for a term which may extend to ten years, or with fine, or with both.

316. *Causing death of quick unborn child by act amounting to culpable homicide:* Whoever does any act under such circumstances, that if he thereby caused death he would be guilty of culpable homicide, and does by such act cause the death of a quick unborn child, shall be punished with imprisonment of either description for a term which may extend to ten years, and shall also be liable to fine.

Illustration: A, knowing that he is likely to cause the death of a pregnant woman, does an act which, if it caused the death of a woman, would amount to culpable homicide. The woman is injured, but does not die; but the death of an unborn quick child with which she is pregnant is thereby caused. A is guilty of the offence defined in this Section.

317. *Exposure and abandonment of child under twelve years, by parent or person having care of it:* Whoever being the father or mother of a child under the age of twelve years, or having the care of such child, shall expose or leave such child in any place with the intention of wholly abandoning such child, shall be punished with imprisonment of either description for a term which may extend to seven years, or with fine, or with both.

Explanation: This section is not intended to prevent the trial of the offender for murder or culpable homicide, as the case may be, if the child dies in consequence of the exposure.

318. *Concealment of birth by secret disposal of dead body:* Whoever, by secretly burying or otherwise disposing of the dead body of a child whether such child dies before or after or during its birth, intentionally conceals or endeavours to conceal the birth of such child, shall be punished with imprisonment of either description for a term which may extend to two years, or with fine, or with both.

11. Gazette of India, Pt. II, Section 2, Extraordinary, dated November 17, 1969, p. 880.
12. Sections 3, 4 and 5 of Medical Termination of Pregnancy Act read as under:

3. *When pregnancies may be terminated by registered medical practitioners:* (1) Notwithstanding anything contained in the Indian Penal Code (45 of 1860), a registered medical practitioner shall not be guilty of any offence under that Code or under any other law for the time being in force, if any pregnancy is terminated by him in accordance with the provisions of this Act.

(2) Subject to the provisions of sub-section (4), a pregnancy may be terminated by a registered medical practitioner,

(a) where the length of the pregnancy does not exceed twelve weeks, if such medical practitioner is, or
(b) where the length of the pregnancy exceeds twelve weeks but does not exceed twenty weeks, if not less than two registered medical practitioners are, of opinion, formed in good faith, that
(i) the continuance of the pregnancy would involve a risk to the life of the pregnant woman or of grave injury to her physical or mental health; or

(ii) there is a substatinal risk that if the child were born, it would suffer from such physical or mental abnormalities as to be seriously handicapped.

Explanation I: Where any pregnancy is alleged by the pregnant woman to have been caused by rape, the anguish caused by such pregnancy shall be presumed to constitute a grave injury to the mental health of the pregnant woman.

Explanation II: Where any pregnancy occurs as a result of failure of any device method used by any married woman or her husband for the purpose of limiting the number of children, the anguish caused by such unwanted pregnancy may be presumed to constitute a grave injury to the mental health of the pregnant woman.

(3) In determining whether the continuance of a pregnancy would involve such risk of injury to the health as is mentioned in sub-section (2), account may be taken of the pregnant woman's actual or reasonably foreseeable environment.

(4) (a) No pregnancy of a woman, who has not attained the age of eighteen years, or, who, having attained the age of eighteen years, is a lunatic, shall be terminated except with the consent in writing of her guardian.

(b) Save as otherwise provided in clause (a), no pregnancy shall be terminated except with the consent of the pregnant woman.

4. *Place where pregnancy may be terminated:* No termination of pregnancy shall be made in accordance with this Act at any place other than

(a) a hospital established or maintained by Government, or
(b) a place for the time being approved for the purpose of this Act by Government.

5. *Sections 3 and 4 when not to apply:* (1) The provisions of Section 4, and so much of the provisions of sub-section (2) of Section 3 as relate to the length of the pregnancy and the opinion of not less than two registered medical practitioners, shall not apply to the termination of a pregnancy by a registered medical practitioner in a case where he is of opinion, formed in good faith, that the termination of such pregnancy is immediately necessary to save the life of the pregnant woman.

(2) Notwithstanding anything contained in the Indian Penal Code (45 of 1860), the termination of a pregnancy by a person who is not a registered medical practitioner shall be an offence punishable under that Code, and that Code shall, to this extent, stand modified.

Explanation: For the purposes of this section, so much of the provisions of clause (d) of Section 2 as relate to the possession, by a registered medical practitioner of experience or training in gynaecology and obstetrics shall not apply.

13. Clause (e) and (f) respectively of Art. 39 of the Constitution.
14. Section 112 of the Evidence Act reads as under:

112. *Birth during marriage, conclusive proof of legitimacy:* The fact that any person was born during the continuance of a valid marriage between his mother and any man, or within two hundred and eighty days after the dissolution, the mother remaining unmarried, shall be conclusive proof

that he is legitimate son of that man, unless it can be shown that the parties to the marriage had no access to each other at any time when he could have been begotten."

15. *Smt. Dukhtar Jahan* v. *Md. Farooquee,* AIR 1987 SC 1049.
16. *Vasu* v. *Santhia,* (1975) KLT 533.
17. Relevant portion of Section 125 Cr. P.C., 1973 reads as under:
125. *Order for maintenance of wives, children and parents:* (1) If any person having sufficient means neglects or refuses to maintain-

(a) his wife, unable to maintain herself, or
(b) his legitimate or illegitimate minor child whether married or not, unable to maintain itself, or
(c) his legitimate or illegitimate child (not being a married daughter) who has attained majority, where such child is, by reason of any physical or mental abnormality or injury unable to maintain itself, or
(d) his father or mother, unable to maintain himself or herself,

A Magistrate of the First class may, upon proof of such neglect or refusal, order such person to make a monthly allowance for the maintenance of his wife or such child, father or mother, as such monthly rate not exceeding five hundred rupees in the whole, as such Magistrate thinks fit, and to pay the same to such person as the Magistrate may, from time to time direct:

Provided that the Magistrate may order the father of a minor female child referred to in Clause (b) to make such allowance, until she attains her majority, if the Magistrate is satisfied that the husband of such minor female child, if married, is not possessed of sufficient means.

18. *Sardar Anoop Singh* v. *The State of U.P. & Another*, I(1995) CCR 30.
19. *Abdulla* v. *The State of Gujarat,* AIR 1988 Guj. 141.
20. Section 20 of the Hindu Succession Act, 1956 reads as under:-
20. *Right of a child in womb:* A child who was in the womb at the time of the death of an intestate and who is subsequently born alive shall have the same right to inherit to the intestate as if he or she had been born before the death of the intestate, and the inheritance shall be deemed to vest in such a case with effect from the death of the intestate.
21. Mullah's Principle of Mohammadan Law (19th Edition) by M. Hidayatullah (former Chief Justice of India) and A. Hidayatullah quoted by Awadh K. Singh in "Alienating a Minor's Estate under Islamic Law", Times of India, dated 28.1.1996 (Delhi Edition).
22. Section 118 of the Evidence Act, 1972 reads as under:

118. *Who may testify*: All persons shall be competent to testify unless the Court considers that they are prevented from understanding the questions put to them, or from giving rational answers to those questions, by tender years, extreme old age, disease, whether of body or mind, or any other cause, of the same kind.

Explanation: A lunatic is not incompetent to testify, unless he is prevented by his lunacy from understanding the questions put to him and giving rational answers to them.

Chapter III

SCHOOLING A CHILD

3.01 Introduction

Chapter IV of the Constitution of India (Arts. 36–51) relates to the '*Directive Principles of State Policy*'. Art. 45 in it, makes provision for free and compulsory education for children up to the age of 14 years, within a period of ten years from the commencement of the Constitution. The Constitution was adopted on the 26th day of November 1949 and as such there should have been total literacy in the country by now. It is, however, a sobering thought that by 2000 A.D. 50 per cent of the world's illiterates will be in India, if requisites steps are not taken.[1] The position can be looked at from a different angle; viz, more than 50 per cent of 330 million children still fall outside the gamut of education. Of these, more than half drop outs of school before they complete the Vth Grade level. Of the remaining, many drop outs in the 8th, 10th and 11th Grades. Not many work towards higher education.[2]

Right of a child to receive free education up to the age of 14 years may not be a fundamental right but since it figures in the Constitution of India, it constitutes the moral responsibility of the society and the Government to redeem the situation that forced the child to give up studies at the school level.

3.02 Early Education

A child education commences with induction to nursery classes where entry is obtained on the basis of admission tests besides exhorbitant charges including capitation fees. A survey conducted by the National Council of Education Research and Training (NCERT) has revealed that hardly 3 per cent of the schools in the

National Capital Region admit children without subjecting them to the ordeal of tests and only 10 per cent of the schools have adopted the play-way system of teaching and learning and 90 per cent of the Kindergarten Schools are no more gardens but kill-joy institutions. They are, in fact, torture cells, where children are expected to cram facts which have the least appeals for them at that stage. Thus, a lot is taught but only very little is understood. The senseless regimen of cramming has indeed become the bane of the modern-day schooling. Such is the rat-race to achieve excellence that our toddlers have to burn the midnight oil at a tender age, although education at that stage should be child-oriented commensurate with the age of the child, his interests and capability. They need to play, enjoy the childhood, spend carefree time before being yoked to the treadmill of examination and competitive tests leading to their life-long subjugation of job-oriented competitive pressures.[3]

3.03 Primary Education—Role and Objectives

Education at the primary level is basically a transmission of cultural heritage which includes instructions in the mother tongue. Generally all instructions at the primary level is in mother tongue. However, the situation with children in our country is that they have to devote more time to the learning of languages as compared to the students of other countries. Every student is required to learn his mother tongue, national language, that is; Hindi and the language of the erstwhile ruler, that is; English. The creative ability of our children is generally assessed in English and his competency in that language.[4]

Education should subscribe to the development of every aspect of human personality—physical, emotional, moral, ethical, intellectual and aesthetic. The aim should be to equip an individual to successfully face the realities of life and take care of the problems faced by him. He should be an asset to the society and should be able to communicate and interact with the people on a human level, to acquire attitudes and personality traits which can equip him to play a positive, meaningful role in the social life of the community. The human personality has many dimensions. The role of education is not only to enrich those but also to strike a happy harmony among them. All these cannot be achieved by class room teachings only.[5]

The common sight in any metropolitan town or big cities is that children properly dressed are found moving with heavy load of books contained in a school bag, the posture being somewhat in bent form on account of the heavy load of books and the movement is towards the school either on foot or to a school transport. In 1995, the Education Minister of Delhi had announced a reduction in the number of days of holidays, obviously with the idea of providing more time for classroom teaching. This, however, is the shrunken view of education, as education is not mere classroom instruction. The horizon of education extends far beyond the classroom and embraces, among others, extra-curricular activities including outdoor and indoor games and cultural activities. In order to achieve the best and appropriate results and proper utilisation of time, the following may, perhaps, be ensured:

(i) The school administration should be strengthened through appointment of full time capable principal or headmaster and teachers who should be in position due to merit and not on any consideration, whatsoever. No appointment should be made on the basis of political or caste considerations.

(ii) The classes should be made to run full-time and no class be missed. It should be ensured that teacher enters the classroom in time and is fully prepared for the subject to be taught on the day.

(iii) The students should regularly be assigned homework and the teachers should regularly check the homework done and mistakes and corrections should be made known to the students.

(iv) The headmaster or the principal should take personal interests in games and see that games should constitute integral part of the school curriculum. The author is reminded of Father Moren of Patna St. Xavier's School who used to go to the playground of the school and play cricket with the students. A European Principal of Patna College used to be present in the field with a whistle in his mouth after college hours and make students play football or hockey or volleyball, the principal himself rendering services as an umpire.

(v) Academic and cultural activities like essay and debate competitions and occasional holding of cultural functions like music, drama etc. should be encouraged. Unfortunately in the name of cultural activities, the schools now-a-days organise fete or *melas* and entrust ticket books to the students and ask them to raise funds by that. In consequence, the priority for the students becomes to approach 'uncles' and 'aunts' who could purchase those tickets. At times the students are not in a position to get the required number of aunts and uncles with the result that many a parents purchase the left over tickets and pay for the same to prevent the child from being humiliated or suffer from a complex and this becomes an extra load on the parents' resources. This is without any benefit to the student himself. This is high time that the Education Departments of the State or the Central Government should think of stopping this practice, if possible through a legislation making penal provisions for such acts of the school authorities including teachers and principals.

3.04 Parental Pressure

A large chunk of school children come from middle class families and every child born in such families raises the hope disproportionate to the capabilities of the child. They are considered by the parents as having extra-ordinary merit and should, therefore, perform extra-ordinarily in days to come not realising that there are limitations. We need to provide unconditional love and support to our children as only in the environment of total acceptance can they bloom. Mrs. Savita Sukhdev Sawhney[6] records a case of a 3 year Geeta, a cute girl attending a neighbourhood play school, run by two sensible sisters, who had been handling kids with love at that stage of their life and never assigned homework to the children. Geeta's mother came to school one day and insisted that her child be given some written work every day. Though they did not like the idea but upon the insistence of the mother, the child was given some homework. When Geeta came to school the next day, she was seen to have burn marks on her hand. She innocently told that her mother had burnt her hand with a match-stick on account of her incapability to do homework.

This happened probably because the mother was overambitious and had overestimated her daughter's capability and in an attempt to see that she goes ahead of everybody and in this effort, she broke the child. The children need their parents and guardians physically and emotionally when they are small and once they have grown and are in their teens, they need space to grow, evolve and blossom into happy healthy beings and it is possible only when the parents do not suffocate them with their own expectations.

3.05 Teaching through Torture

"Spare the rod, spoil the child" is an old maxim. It is meant primarily to correct a child, if necessary by the application of stick, which should be used as a means to achieve the goal of preventing a child from getting spoilt and not to cause any physical harm to the tiny tots. But instances are there that, at times, there are indiscriminate beating of the child in schools and at home resulting in tragic incidents. The following are quoted by way of example:

A mathematics teacher of Oxford Senior Secondary School Vikaspuri, Delhi is reported to have slapped ten students of Class X, allegedly in anger against them for not bringing compass as per direction given a day before resulting in loss of hearing of one student inspite of 2½ hour surgery by an E.N.T. specialist in a hospital in order to correct two perforations in eardrum caused by the slapping.[7]

A five year girl lost vision in one eye on being spanked by the teacher. According to a news item, in Japan, a student was beaten by a teacher which ,caused his death. In U.S., a mother, presumably on account of her annoyance with her children, put her two children in a car, secured them with safety belts, drove the vehicle to a lake and pushed it into the lake with the children. An angry father in a rural area in Punjab, caned his sons so severly that the boy collapsed.[8]

Nothing can be more cruel than merciless beating of a weak and defenceless child. By doing so, not only the child is crippled physically but also gets disturbed mentally. What is created in the process is not the correction of the child but turning him into a physical and mental wreck.

The episode of child beating is not confined to any restricted group but is inherent in all the sections of the society, poor or rich, literate or illeterate. Poverty stricken society records a large number of brutalities, probably on account of the socio-economic deprivation. In educated class, it may be parental maladjustment, frustration in office or too rigid a code of personal discipline leading to the torture of the child who is readily available to face the traumatic experience from the elders who erroneously believe that they are the custodian of the commodity known as child and are entitled to inflict any treatment of their choice.

Child beating does not involve a slap or two to an erring youngster. In their thoughtless anger elders whip, strangle, flog, famish, hang up-side down or violently bang the child against the wall and after the anger subsides, the erring parents or elders also suffer pangs of remorse.

At one time, the problem assumed such distressing dimension that a Society for Prevention of Cruelty to Children was established to conduct periodic surveys to the problems of the children.

A battered and humiliated child often loses the sense of shame and indignation and in course of time develops immunity to any punishment and becomes defiant. A slow psychic death takes place that results in immeasurable personality deficiency. Boys turn into hardened criminals or become obsessed individuals depending upon their social and familial circumstance, while girls may become neurotic or sexually frigid and suffer maladjustment in later life.

Corporal punishment, as a means, for maintaining discipline or for improving the learning ability of the child is not a necessity. In dealing with a child, the idea should be to instill a sense of righteousness into the erring student and other on-looking students as this lays the foundation stone for leading a successful life in times to come. Right punishment inflicted in a right manner and at the right moment to a defaulting student is one which is bravely accepted by the wrong-doer. This is possible, provided the punishing teacher explains to the punished boy as to the breaking of rule causes harm to the student community in general. The child should not get the idea that he is a culprit but his action amounts to omission or default.

Corporal punishment can deliver the goods if the teacher, who resorts to it, has earned the respect of the students. There may be a situation where defaulting students are not ready to receive punishment and no volunteer comes either. In that event, the only chance of correcting the erring chap is through observing penance, for his misdeeds of breaking rules, is by the teacher himself.[9]

In dealing with children, therefore, parents and teachers must be considerate, sober and very slow in inflicting corporal punishments.[10]

3.06 National Policy on Education

The National Policy on Education, 1986, known as the New Education Policy was evolved in 1986. In 1992, a National Advisory Committee on Education was constituted by the Ministry of Human Resource Department under the Chairmanship of Professor Yashpal and its terms of reference had been:[11]

> "to advise on the ways and means to reduce the load on school students at all levels particularly the young students while improving quality of learning and skill formation."

The Yashpal Committee after analysing the existing scenario has pointed out that both the teacher and the child have lost the joy in teaching and learning respectively. The parents, teachers and the children are consistently undei the awe of examination results and the percentage of marks that is obtained in examination. For the administration of education, the key words remains the prescribed syllabus. On the other hand, it is the curriculum which reflects the expected learning. Learning in school should be aimed at preparing the child to understand the environment around him, to perceive the changes that are taking place all over and are likely to take place in future. He also has to identify his own role in these changes. Development of necessary skills should constitute a part of changing scenario in terms of perception, participation and utilisation. Education should make a person, capable of developing the capacity of appreciating and respecting the bounty of nature, the miracles created by it and develop reverence to the natural world and the dignity of law. This could be achieved only when the learning focusses on development of skills and the required competency. The curriculum must respond to the emerging needs and priorities of the society. Under the present situation, some of the critical factors, relevant to the curriculum are the population growth, changing life-style, removal of disparities, emerging role of women, social integration and cohesion, economic restructuring, advent of new technology etc. The curriculum is an ever changing process and should continue to absorb these changes. It should be consistent with the needs of the society which the pupil is likely to face in his future life. Here lies the crux of the problem and its criticality in respect of the development of curriculum.

The 1986 Policy has carefully stipulated development of district level resource centres. The District Institute of Education and Training (DIETs) is required to make functional at the earliest. One of the branches identified in these institutions is the Curriculum and the Material Development Branch. The process of curriculum development must begin in these institutions for the primary and elementary stage. This may, perhaps, be one of the feasible approaches to reduce the load on the young learners, presently crushed under the overload of the prescription of mechanically constituted syllabi and mad rush for the percentage of marks and disproportionately high expectations from parents. The phenomena common to developing countries is the lack of literacy among a large percentage of the population. Inspite of the declared purposes of the South Asian Governments to give priorities to the elementary school education to achieve total literacy level, secondary schools are rising faster and tertiary schools even more faster although the latter is more expensive.[12]

3.07 Primary Education and the Government

The Government of India has asserted before the Supreme Court of India that by the year 1991, it has provided primary schools within one km distance to 8.26 lakh habitation containing about 94 per cent of the population, in effect the enrolment rates had gone up in eightees and had approximated to 100 per cent at the primary stage.[13] In order to achieve the target of Universal Elementary Education (UEE), the State Governments have abolished the tuition fees at the primary stage in the Government sponsored institutions. There is, however, another side of the story, that is; the steady fall in the share of total outlay for Elementary Education from 56 per cent in the First Plan to 30 per cent in the Fourth Plan and upward trend in the share of University Education.[13]

The Lokshala Project for Universalisation of Elementary Education, quoting from the Ministry's Annual Report of 1993-94 points out drop-out rates are significant, retention of students in schools is low and wastage. There are striking disparities in access to Elementary Education—disparities as between regions, rural and urban areas, boys and girls, and the haves and have-nots.[14]

3.08 Education for Rural Children[15]

Although, as per assertion of the Government, there exists a primary school within one km of every village but what is the school? The building is with a shabby up-keep, poor resources and dissatisfied teachers whose rural posting was against their wishes. The general picture of schools in rural areas is rather grim. Therefore, the children of rich peasants opt out for urban schools where they join and study along with urban students coming from middle class families. The children of the poor, having no other alternative attend such schools.

Every system of teaching has the system of examination to test the knowledge of the student and his eligibility for promotion to the next higher class. In most of the rural schools nearly 80 per cent of the examinees fail in 10th or 12th class. Failed students lower the morale of those studying, making education in a rural school unattractive.

At the primary level, we have different story to tell. In order to boost school retention, every child, irrespective of his eligibility is promoted to the next higher class. This has led to disasterous results. The teaching is without any accountability towards performance by the teacher and the student alike. According to Krishna Kumari,[15] a peasant woman who came to Tikamgarh Children Literate Centre (CLC) meeting said that her son had passed the Vth Grade but cannot read or write.

At a meeting of the parents whose children are attending a project on alternative primary education at Tikamgarh Children Literate Centre (CLC), a peasant woman brought to light the picture of her village primary school and vividly described the apathy of the two teachers and their cruelty which found expression in the beatings, the children received. She further pointed out that if her child had a stomach ache, instead of taking care of his physical sufferings the teachers hurled abuses. That was precisely the cause of her withdrawing the child from the village primary school.

The rural schools are, thus, classical examples of neglect and exhibit how the lack of proper planning affects the children education at the initial stage of learning.

3.09 Conclusion

The universalisation of elementary education in its totality remains an elusive goal with much ground to be covered. In order to improve the quality of education one has to look into the grass-root problems. Specific solutions or remedies have to be found out for the peculiar problems of each area for which surveys have to be conducted. Such surveys are significant and would give insight into the question of retention level of education of primary school children.[16]

REFERENCES

1. Kavita A. Sharma, "More snakes than ladder", *The Hindustan Times* (Delhi Edn.), dated August 29, 1995.
2. Sunil Batra, "The thankless job of teachers", *The Times of India* (Delhi Edn.) dated 6.9.95.
3. Ash Narain Roy, "Education by torture", *The Hindustan Times* (Delhi Edn.), dated September 1, 1995.
4. K.K. Khullar, "Balancing the cultural education", *The Hindustan Times* (Delhi Edn.), dated 10.10.95.
5. Niti Paul Mehta, "Need for quality time in school", *The Hindustan Times* (Delhi Edn.), dated 11.7.1995.
6. Savita Sukhdev Sawhney, "Parental pressures break the child", *The Hindustan Times* (Delhi Edn.), dated 24.1.1995.
7. Parul Chandra, "Slapping causes loss of hearing", *The Hindustan Times* (Delhi Edn.), dated 29.10.95
8. Usha Pandey, "You hurt me, because I am small", *The Hindustan Times* (Delhi Edn.), dated 29.895
9. S.G. Manipilli, "Use the rod sparingly", *The Hindustan Times* (Delhi Edn.), dated 29.8.95.
10. Usha Pandey, "You hurt me, because I am small", *The Hindustan Times* (Delhi Edn.), dated 29.8.95.
11. J.S. Rajput, "Curriculum should not be a burden", *The Hindustan Times* (New Delhi Edn.), dated June 6, 1995.
12. Gunnar Mridal, "*Asian Drama*".
13. *J.P. Unnikrishnan* v. *The State of A.P., AIR 1933 SC 2178.*
14. Savita A. Sharma, "More Snakes than Ladder", *The Hindustan Times (Delhi Edn.), dated 29.8.95.*
15. Krishna Kumar, "Rural children—Fighting the educational bias", *Times of India,* dated 1.2.95
16. Anil Nayar, "Enough funds, but no attention", *The Hindustan Times* (Delhi Edn.), dated May 1, 1995.

Chapter IV

POST SCHOOL EDUCATION

4.01 Introduction

After completing 10+2, those students who can afford or intend to pursue higher education seek admission to a college in any one of the three faculties; Arts, Commerce or Science or some professional course like Engineering, Medical or Law or a Polytechnic. For admission to any professional course in a college, the student has to take chance through competitive examinations, often held as Combined Competitive Tests. Nearly 50 per cent of the seats are reserved for O.B.C. and SC/ST categories and in this category those securing even poor marks are entitled to score over those brilliant students coming under the general categories. Most of the students, who fail to secure a seat at this stage, on account of the seats under the reserved category, get frustrated. The position is that, the moment 10+2 examination ends, the students start preparing for their Competitive Examinations. The students do not get any breathing time or any time for relaxation and go in a state of tension. The question is what is the importance of Secondary Board Examination or the utility of good results exhibited at these examinations? Why not admissions to these institutions be on the basis of marks secured at 10+2 examination? The answer is very simple. In a vast country like India, having a population exceeding 900 millions, all examinations are not held with the same standard and with the same strictness in invigilation and with the same standard of marking or evaluation system. Although it is not impossible to enforce a uniform system, this is not resorted to. A burning example is the teaching through the C.B.S.E. course throughout the country holding examinations through a common question and evaluation by the same standard.

4.02 Joy and Pains of College Initiation

After a student passes his school examination and takes admission in a college, he has the joy of becoming a college student. The author, after he took admission in one of the prestigious colleges of Patna University in 1942, was told by his father that from the date he has taken admission in the college he has become a college student and that was a moment of happiness for him. The college opened on 1.7.1942 and teaching started in the institution from the first period of the first day. Now-a-days, a student has to run about in various colleges for admission at the pre-admission stage and after the college has opened, he has the trauma of ragging which continues till the Students Union Elections are over and quite a good amount of valuable time is lost in these. Politics is ingrained into the veins of a student at this immature stage and the students right track at this time gets deviated into caste and party politics.

4.03 Ragging

Ragging may be defined as the outbrust of organised horseplay, usually in defiance of authority against undergraduates, in practice, it is bullying of freshers.[1] Ragging may be decent, indecent or ugly. It started in the Western countries by way of fun intended for introduction and while it is a way out for fun in the West it is becoming indecent, and/or ugly leading to fatality and ending in many tragic incidents. It is changing from simple fun to sadism.[1]

Ragging commences as soon as a student approaches a college for submitting application forms and it invariably starts with the senior asking the *'Fachcha'* (*Fachcha* means Fresher Plus Bachcha): "Why do you like to join this college?" If the poor fresher says 'No', pat comes the question, 'Why?' and if he says, 'yes', he/she is asked for an introduction and if the fresher is lucky, he/she is let off.

The second place of ragging is the University Special Bus wherein the *'Fachcha'* is asked to introduce him/herself, his/her hobbies, the course undertaken for studies and/or to perform a dance or sing a song. The plea in favour of this, which is put forward is this that it helps to break the barrier between seniors and freshers, and also it develops into friendship.

The third place of ragging is the campus, canteen and the lawns. First of all this is the dress code, which is nothing but an array of mismatched clothings plus oily hair, is dictated. The fresher may be asked to sing a popular film song or to perform some dance sequence. At the close of the episode, he may be treated with *'samosa'* or hot or cold drinks. Usually those who intend to stand as a candidate in Students Union Elections take a word of assurance that the student will vote for them and promise to help them as and when approached and required.

4.04 Criminal Ragging

The incidents of ragging in some instances have attained the stage of criminality. Physical and mental tortures are frequent. Stripping of a girl student in Delhi University has been reported in recent times. There is also the report that an engineering student was pushed from the hostel roof because he declined to take drugs. In a college from Uttar Pradesh, a girl student was sent to the Boys Hostel in the evening, as a part of ragging, on the pretext of delivering a book. She is reported to be missing since then. Inspite of several judicial enquiries and students strike there, nothing has come out and the case remains shrouded in mystery.[2]

In hostels, two procedures are very popular. The fresher, is made to stand upside down with his head in a commode which is flushed. This is called 'brain-wash'. The second is the candle dance, which is strip-tease, albeit the male version.[2]

Medical college freshers are subjected to more inhuman treatment in ragging. Often a fresher is locked up in mortuary for hours together by seniors till he is scared to death. Yet in another case reported from a medical college, a girl student died due to shock treatment from ragging. In that incident when a girl student attempted to act smart, a senior student, in order to teach a lesson to her for her smartness, cut an arm from a dead body and placed the same on the top of the door of a laboratory. As soon as the fresher opened the door, the arm fell on her, in consequence of which, she went into deep shock and she died in the next couple of days. In the same campus, a fresher, who refused to submit herself to ragging was made to sleep on an almirah top and later portions of her body was burnt with lighted cigarette ends. She was, after that, hospitalised.

These two tragic incidents have finally put an end to ragging practice in that institution.[2]

The story of one medical institution is that a fresher was sent by his senior to the Post-mortem Section. There he saw a skeleton with luminated eyes and flourescent hands that appeared to be moving on their own volitions. It was the handiwork of a senior student. In another case a student was made to stand on the weak over-hanging edge of a window on the second floor of the hostel building on a cold winter night. The student was admitted to the hospital with multiple fractures when he slipped from the perch.[3] The list of ragging is endless. Ragging has become a matter of worry for freshers and their parents and guardians.[3] The ugly incidents from the hostels are not brought to light as the freshers have to live in the same hostel with the seniors, who will make it a point to take revenge upon the complainant.

The trauma of ragging in professional colleges is reflected in the poor results of the students in the first semester, which is the ragging period. Many students, give up their studies for fear of ragging. Some break down under the pressure of ragging. There are reports that students have committed suicide in consequence of severe ragging.

Ragging is being continued from year to year in consequence of a chain reaction because a student once ragged as a fresher, utilises the best of the opportunity to satisfy his mauled ego and participates in ragging freshers of his time.[4] On account of the immaturity, he does not look to the traumatic part of it and does not suggest any reform or refrain from indulging in it.

College and hostel authorities of an institution should put down ragging with a firm hand and take stern disciplinary action against such students who indulge in ragging. The teachers should start teaching right from the first day and the first period. Politics and political influence should not be allowed to pollute the academic climate of the college and the universities and Students Unions should be banned. In author's (K.K.) time, half a decade ago, there used to be only academic and cultural activities in colleges and the working office-bearers were usually nominated by the respective professors and hardly there used to be any dispute or controversy because both for the teacher and the students, teaching found a place of prime importance.

4.05 Falling Standard of Teaching

Teaching is very exciting provided the teachers are both innovative and allowed to frame the syllabi in the light of new developments. In the present day scenario, most of the teachers tend to offer more or less the same courses over the years and simply become agents of transferring the same idea from year to year. Thus, they lose the capacity to think afresh. The students also become victim of this process and they devise short cut methods to secure marks even without the grasp of the fundamental principles of the discipline. This is a serious problem as the students in the existing situation can answer questions without attending classes and without any contact with the teachers.

The reasons for falling standard in teaching are under:

(i) *Lack of interest in teaching*: For a variety of reasons, the teaching job is not attractive. Given a chance, most of the teachers would prefer other profession like administrative jobs and bureaucrat's status.

(ii) *Teaching only as a means of livelihood*: Since a large number of teachers take up teaching job as a means of earning livelihood, the teachers are frequently hunting foreign assignment birds' and at the slightest opportunity go abroad to earn money in foreign currencies. It has been found that teachers have gone even to those countries from where they are sent back to India immediately after their term is over. Whatever the teacher has contributed in that institution is ignored.[5]

(iii) *Political appointment in teaching jobs*: Many a time appointment to teaching jobs are made on political considerations. Merit, ability and aptitude are completely ignored.

(iv) *Disinterested Research Workers*: Since independence, research activities have increased but suffers enormously due to disinterested research scholars. The University toppers, who usually are selected for research work, have no interest and they use the research assignments to serve the triple purposes, viz; providing a place in the hostel for stay; library facilities and subsistence allowance by way of scholarship. The moment a student succeeds in his attempt to secure a job elsewhere suited to his choice, he leaves his research work in the middle. It is only when he does not get a job and has become over-age that he attempts to complete his research work.

(v) *Appointment of teachers on regional basis*: Although Ph.D. is prescribed as the qualification for appointment to the post of a lecturer, even the Central Universities appoint mere M.Sc./M.A. from their own Universities. If a Ph.D. from another University has applied for the post he is being rejected only on the basis of not having been an ex-student of that University.

4.06 Adoption of Unfair Means in Examination

On 28.11.1995, a Division Bench of Patna High Court, on a Public Interest Petition, passed an order prohibiting holding of examinations in all the Universities of Bihar except that of Patna University till further direction by the court. This step was taken to prevent the large scale use of unfair means in examinations conducted by Universities and institutions connected with the Universities. Patna University was spared on account of its proximity to the State capital where supervision work in examination was entrusted to advocates appointed by the High Court. As a protest against this order, demonstrations were staged by students at various places, both urban and rural in the State.

On the following day, i.e., on 29th November, 1995, while amending the order of the previous day's order, the High Court passed an order that test examination, semester examination and practical examinations be held. Perhaps no body brought to the notice of the Hon'ble Court that the system of conducting internal examination was non-existent since the last several decades and whatever was being done was by way of meeting the formality. In practical examinations, there is such a co-ordination between the examiners and examinees that such examinations are shown to be successfully held even in those institutions where no laboratory exists. The Division Bench in this context passed two orders, viz;

(i) the answer papers of the examinations conducted by Patna University be sealed, and
(ii) imposition of ban on the appointment of examiners.

Further the Vice-Chancellors have been asked to suggest in their Universities necessary reforms.[6]

As a sequel to the orders of the Hon'ble High Court, the University Administration in Bihar are bound to hold examinations with due strictness. Students of Patna University are adamant that if other Universities openly allow the use of unfair means in examination, then why a ban on the use of unfair means in examination be imposed on the students of Patna University only. Their plea is that in other Universities, the students are allowed to take blank answer books to their houses and submit written answer books. In Patna University, at least the students should be allowed to use unfair means in examination halls.

The spokesman of striking students said that students do not favour use of unfair means but the Universities and college authorities should enforce the following conditions:

(i) Completion of the course within the academic session;
(ii) A minimum of 180 days of teaching in colleges; and
(iii) the presence of teachers at least for four hours in college on each working day.[7]

The rot in examination system cannot be taken in isolation. It has political, social, financial, cultural and several other factors to influence this. Although it appears that this is growing out of the collusion between the teachers and students but several others; such as; guardians, police, administration and so many are involved in it and are responsible for its growth. It is for the State administration to see that the proper climate in academic institutions be introduced and enforced. So long it is not done it is an offence against the future generation who is at the formative stage. Such offence may not be as per definition of any Act but in effect it is against their interests.

4.07 Callousness in Evaluation and Revaluation of Answer Books

Annual examinations are the only means by which the potential and performance of a student is judged. A great caution, therefore, is required in evaluation of answer papers as well as the Examination Department should exercise vigilance to see that no answer papers are missed. But how this is done in Universities will be clear from a few examples from the Prestigious Central University in the Capital city of the country.

(i) Ram Tanaya Ratnam, a student of Hons. in Statistics in Hindu College was awarded Zero in one paper and marked absent in two papers although the student claimed that he appeared in all the three papers and had done well.[8]
(ii) Ajay Varma, a student of English Hons. in Khalsa College, Delhi, was horrified to find that he had been marked absent

in paper VII, inspite of the fact that he had appeared. After receiving his marks sheet on Aug. 24, he made a representation against this discrepancy. His attendance in the examination was verified.

On September 1, 1995, he received his revised Marks Sheet and he found that he had been awarded only 45 marks in Paper VII, the answer book of the same was missed. The Experts and Senior teachers pointed out that Varma's case is categorised under "Copy Missing Case" and in such a situation he should have been awarded the average of two best answer books of his and in his case this works out to 58.

On account of the callous attitude of the examination Department of the University, Varma not only had to pass through a mental trauma but he could not secure admission in M.A. English which ruined his career.[9]

(iii) A girl student, who was a brilliant one, committed suicide as inspite of having worked very hard, she secured unexpetedly very low marks in examination. Perhaps the authorities could realise this disappointment and depression that follow when a student secures poor marks which, at times, lead to disastrous results.[10]

Though the Delhi University offers solution to the problem of poor results by making provision for getting the answer papers revalued but this provision is not of much value. The shock of poor results upsets the students and revaluation makes the situation worse. It has been the experience of the students that in revaluation marks get reduced. This is a common complaint. Some students do not depose any faith in revaluation as they have the experience that revaluation means simply re-totalling of marks. Still the greater shock emanates when a hard-working student learns that his class mate who was never a regular student could secure better marks by the procedure of guide-study for a month or so. All these show that the examination system is neither fool-proof nor reliable.

4.08 Correspondence Coaching

Those students, who either do not get admission in regular courses or are not interested in attending classes as commuting itself is a tiring exercise, resort to taking admissions in Correspondence

Courses. In this system course materials are sent to students by post. Studying at home throws the focus of a daily time schedule entirely on the students. Most students in Correspondence Courses work as well as manage to make good use of their time. This places a greater sense of responsibility on a student, and encourages problem solving skills since they have to workout solutions to querries themselves. Since qualified academicians are involved in preparing the course material, standards are generally high. However, studying through post involves total dependency on the postal system which is not a reliable means. Postal strike, delays, misplaced parcels rules the study of a student of Correspondence Course. It is reported that most courses at Indira Gandhi National Open University (IGNOU) were delayed this year (1995) as the number of parcels to be posted far exceeded the availability of Mail Bags.

A delayed receipt of study material results in students rushing through the course in order to keep up with the various dates for the submission of assignments.

IGNOU has grown in popularity over the past couple of years on account of no ban on the age of enrolment and an adequate duration to complete the course makes these courses convenient for working students. The School of Correspondence Studies and continuing education is the obvious alternative to DU. One drawback of the system is that there is a limited number of seats making entrance to this course dependent on availability and luck.[11]

4.09 Vocational Education

Vocational education imparts practical training to a student in a particular occupational field. It embraces many attractive courses on Computers, Secretarial Practices, Emboriodery, Textile Designing, Fashion Technology, Interior Decoration and charge very high fees. Many such institutions do not have adequate essential equipments like typewriters, computers etc. Pratibha Punj,[12] publishes a newspaper report about the International Polytechnic for Women, supposed to be one of the premier prestigious institution for vocational training for women, which claims to offer vocational training to women to make them self-dependent.

Although the institution announces some hi-fi courses, it is not properly equipped. The class-room meant for 25 is stuffed with 45 students. In the Shorthand Class there is not enough tables and the students have to do writing work by keeping their note-books in their laps. Although it claims to impart training in operation of Electronic Typing but hardly there is any such instrument. Even it has not enough Manual Typewriters in proper working order. As regards infra-structure facilities, it has only one toilet for the whole institution, no common room and the hostel facilities are extremely inadequate and a large number of students are crammed in each room. Only the course on textile designing is recognised but other courses are not recognised. Its advertisement on attractive brochures attract students from middle class families. The students on joining feel that they have been entrapped and the parents feel that their hard-earned money has been enticed away.

REFERENCES

1. Anjaja Mitra, "Campus Scenes—A Savage Tradition is Spreading", *The Hindustan Times,* (Delhi Edn.), dated September 11, 1993.
2. Nishtha Langer (D.C.E.), "Sadistic Exercise", *The Hindustan Times,* dated Aug. 2, 1995.
3. Rangeen Singh, "The Pains of College Initiation", *The Hindustan Times,* (Delhi Edn.), dated August 1, 1995.
4. Gyan Lal, "Charming Spell", *Young Life Column, The Hindustan Times,* (Delhi Edn.), dated August 2, 1995.
5. Dr. B. Chakrabarty, "Airport Lecturers, Wayward Students", *Hindustan Times,* (Delhi Edn.), dated November 29, 1995.
6. Rajendra Kishore, "Pariksha Mein Kadachar, Ek Mushkil Hal Ki Talash" (Immorality in examination—search for a difficult solution)", *The Hindustan Times,* (Hindi) (Patna Edn.) dated December 7, 1995.
7. Report by Shri Lakshmikant Sajal from his Patna Office on "Bihar Mein Nakal Rokane Ki Pahal", *Sunday Hindustan* (Hindi) New Delhi, dated December 10, 1995.
8. Ajit Kumar, "Young Life—Unfair Deal", *The Hindustan Times,* (Delhi Edn.) dated August 16, 1995.
9. Hindustan Times Correspondent, "Victims of Varsity Callousness" *The Hindustan Times,* (Delhi Edn.) dated September 9, 1993.
10. Jyoti Madan (Hindu College), "Big Hoax of Revaluation" *The Hindustan Times,* (Delhi Edn.), dated August 16, 1995.
11. Aashish Kumar Sen (IGNOU), "Giving Kate Moss a Complex", *The Hindustan Times,* dated December 6, 1995.
12. Pratibha Punj (IPW) "Classes of Nightmares", *The Hindustan Times,* (Delhi Edn.) dated August 23, 1995.

Chapter V

CHILDREN AND ELECTRONIC MEDIA

5.01 Introduction

On January 10, 1996, the Additional District and Sessions Judge at Barasat (West Bengal) awarded death sentence to two youngsters, Sajal Barui and Ranjit Mondal as Sajal alongwith five of his friends who planned and carried out the murder of his father, Subal Barui, step-mother, Niyati Barui and step-brother, Kajal Barui in a residential apartment of Dum-Dum on November 22, 1993.[1] Four other young boys, Subhrasil Roy, Alok Saha, Samar Saha and Debashis Dey were awarded life sentence. All the convicted persons were in the group of 17–20 years. Sajal, Debashis, Subhrasil and Sumar had confessed to their involvement in the crime in course of their confessional statement recorded under Section 164 Cr.P.C., 1973 before the Judicial Magistrate of Barrackpur.

On the fateful night, the six youngsters assembled near the entrance of the apartment. They were armed with choppers, rubber gloves, a length of rope and black masks. Mrs. Niyati Barui was alone in the flat and watching TV when Sajal tip-toed inside. All his friends except Alok followed him. Alok kept guard at the entrance. Sajal brandished knife to silence his step-mother. She was then dragged to the bedroom and gagged. Her hands and feet were tied to a chair then they looted the almirah and Samar left with a part of the booty.

After sometime, Kajal Barui entered the flat. He was similarly gagged and tied to a post. At around mid-night, Mr. Subal

Barui came and was similarly dealt with. After that Subhrasil left with another instalment of looted property. Sanjit, Ranjit and Debashsis burnt the blood-stained clothes and rubber gloves in order to cause disappearance of evidence. According to one version, they ate thereafter and threw about coins on the center table as a murder maniac was seen to have done in a TV film.

In his statement, Sajal also admitted that he hit upon the murder plan from TV films on violence to which he had become an addict.

The Judge in his 187 page judgement commented on the pernicious influence of sex and violence films on the young minds and asked the Board of Film Censors to think deeply on the issue.

Sixteen year old Rahul (not his real name), now an inmate of a Reformatory School, was forbidden from going out during his examination period and, therefore, he killed his parents, grandparents and sister by giving them sweets laced with a quantity of lethal poison. He is unrepentent and does not offer any explanation.[2]

Three students of Class IX, in Faridabad, hacked to death one of their classmates with a sword. He had refused to stop talking to a girl one of them fancied. All of them are the sons of well-to-do businessmen. They have no regrets.[2]

Cheating in school examination has become wide spread and more often than not invigilators are threatened into submission. In a spine chilling case of bizarre, mindless violence, a girl was dragged out of an examination hall by a group of boys and burnt alive in a school in Maharashtra.[2]

Hooliganism in Universities has shown a steady uptrend in the past few years. Almost every college has its share of '*dadas*' and their respective gangs. Mob mentality rules the roost as does the principle of '*might is right*'. Politics in college life has contributed equally in vitiating the atmosphere. As a matter of fact, during the last few years, the situation has worsened so much that young scholars are scared of joining certain colleges.

Extreme cases of violent ragging are also another cause of anguish to freshers and sophomores alike. Cases of kidnapping, stabbing and roughing up of students and even teachers are common in colleges these days. In a well-known New Delhi South Campus College, a student was shot dead in cold-blood by another student and his goons. The delinquent is the son of a local police officer.[2]

The son of a high ranking police officer, has been charged with the murder of a Delhi University Law student Priyadarshini. A vociferous group of the *'Daughters of Vitasta'*, the women's wing of Panun Kashmir, raised slogan against the Delhi Police and demanded a fair trial and stern punishment of the accused when the accused was brought to the Court of the Metropolitan Magistrate.[3]

Gaurav, a child aged 3 years has just returned from his nursery school and starts playing with WWF figurines and with one deft stroke of his hand he breaks the neck of one of the figurine and says, "I have won". Apparently the beheading does not seem to be signifacent to his parents and is dismissed as child's play.[2]

Shakti Kapoor in a whacky hairdo runs after Aditya Pancholi brandishing a naked sword. In a frenzied state, he hack off the hero's legs with one stroke of the weapon. The children viewers, sit on the edge of their seats and sequel with excitement.[2]

The author saw the other day a little child chasing two other children with an open knife.

In a remote village in Bihar, an eight year old child, during a play killed its three play-mates. According to a published report coming up in December 1994, a four year child had killed a six months' infant through strangulation.[4]

5.02 Blame for Brutalisation of Young Mind

The aforesaid incidents are some of the many which come to notice every day through newspapers. The main question which comes to our mind is who is to be blamed for brutalising the young mind. The reply is the modern electronic media like cinema, television video cassette and above all the Government which has failed to exercise effective control over these. Millions of kids all over India are being fed an overdose of supposedly harmless entertainment; to the extent that they get addicted to it. Gun toting, sword wielding goons and macho heroes dressed in tight jeans, open shirts without any banians are as much in demand as the WWF werstlers. Children, especially boys can be found playing with all sorts of toy-guns and imitating film heroes. The craving for more and more violence does not seem to show any sign of abating. Thrills, spills and chills have become the hall mark of entertainment for kids.[2]

Reel life events are not better than real life in terms of influencing adolescents. With crime rates touching new heights, they are splashed all over the electronic as well as print media.

5.03 Print Media

The colour photographs of the aftermath of Rajiv Gandhi's assassination as published in one news magazine in all their gory details were very well received. What was the most disturbing fact is that the particular issue sold like a hot cake. Similarly a photograph of a policeman carrying the severed head of a bomb-blast victim by its hair appeared on the front page of a daily. In no time of the paper reaching the subscribers, it became the talk of the town.[2]

What is most disturbing and disgusting is that such gory and gruesome details do not affect the common man's sensibilities. When a generation of the adults has accepted violence and mayhem as a part of their lives, it is but natural for the younger generation to follow suit. For instance, the front page of any newspaper must contain one or two violent incidents of death with a host of scattered news of violence, rape, murders etc. in subsequent pages.

Although violence is not an unfamiliar phenomenon since time immemorial, yet it has never been so prevalent and as profound as it is in our society today. The cult of violence has spread its vicious tentacles like a malignant disease and has assumed an incurable malady resulting in the emergence of juvenile delinquency at an acceleratated rate; the children imbibing the cult of violence at an early age.[2]

5.04 Cinema

The face of the cinema has changed radically in the 90s. The excesses crossed all limits of show with dance masters and fight masters outdoing each other in competition to arouse audiences. The extreme forms of brutality shown in the cinema, is so exaggerated as to be unreal. In some cases it is a reflection of the ground reality. The films usually show what is going on around us. Are the politicians, the forces of law and order, the officials and the public servants as pure and above board as they would have us believe? In small and large degrees, violence has invaded our lives along with its side effects like fear, hostility, cynicism, tensions and a sense of insecurity. Not only crimes against women are shown to be committed but actually these are perpetrated with all impunity and the accused persons let off lightly or allowed to go free for want of convincing evidence to prove the case beyond reasonable doubts. Govind Nihlani's *Drohkal*, the award-winning film shows the reality that the forces of law and order are vulnerable to the violence which they are meant to curb. The unexpected overwhelming response to the film titled *Hum Apke Hain Kaun* which depicts an ideal world where kindness, helpfulness and compassion rule. This amply proves that the audiences are now fed up with the heavy dose of violence and sexual antics in mainstream cinema. That the people are ready to accept with open arms the film executed with fineness and a content that invite thought and discussion because it touches heart and real life, This has been proved by the box-office success of the film 'Bombay'.[5]

5.05 Adult Films

With the onset of Television and the fear of implantation of bombs in Cinema halls, the interest of the audience in visiting the cinema touched a new low. Some producers stated making pronorgraphic pictures as paradigms of art. The stinks of these dirty films proved too strong for them to camouflage their sinister designs.

Such films are meant to be shown to the adults only and the words "strictly for adults" are superscribed on them, no restraint is exercised in the display of obscene postures in public places which are frequently seen by those who are not adults. Therefore, if a film is confined to be seen by adults, the display of posters of such films should not be open to the children and adolescents.[6] The display of adult films is not only a penal offence under the provisions of Section 292–294 I.P.C.[7] but it also ultra vires the Constitution. Obscenity is an offence under Section 292 I.P.C., Post Office Act of 1893, the Sea Customs Act 1878, the Dramatic Performance Act, 1876 and the Indecent Representation of Women (Prohibition) Act, 1980.[6] A bookseller in Bombay was punished under Section 292–I.P.C. for selling and keeping for sale the unexpurgated Edition of D.H. Lawrence, "Lady Chatterley's

Lover". The convict came in appeal before the Hon'ble Supreme Court challenging the validity of Section 292 I.P.C. in the context of Article 19 of the Constitution of India. The Apex Court clarified that Article 19 of the Constitution which granted freedom of speech, as well imposes restriction vide its Clause (2) on the exercise of that right in the interest of public order, decency or morality. The Apex Court further ruled that in case of obscene publications, the prosecution was not required to adduce positive evidence to prove mens-rea. Inference in such cases could be drawn, from the overwhelming circumstantial evidence.

The Queen's Bench of England in *Rex* v. *Hicklin* (1868) also held the similar views on the question of obsecenity. Both the Courts agreed that if the impugned matter, whether any publication or a film, has the tendency to deprave and corrupt those whose minds are open to such immoral influences, it can be designated as obscene and the same would invite punishments.

If the Hicklin test is applied to the adult films, it will transpire that each and every such film is obscene and warrants a ban in the larger public interests. Everybody from the producer to the Censor Board should be accountable for the production and exhibition of adult films, thereby indulging in flagrant violation of the constitutional and legal provisions in this regard.

In addition to the above, Article 51A of the Constitution of India enjoins on every citizen to renounce which are outrageous to the dignity of women.

Obscenity is obnoxious not only according to Hindu Shastras and scriptures but also according to other religions practiced in the country. The time has come requiring our joint attention and giving serious thoughts to the burgeoning problems of existing vulgarity and obscenity in films. There should be drastic amendments in Censorship Laws to make them subservient to public morality and social ethos.[6]

5.06 Film Songs

The last decade had seen a spate of vulgar songs with lewd scenes being exhibited on the silver screen. To quote for instance, *Jumma, Jumma, chooma de-de, Choli ke pichchey kya hai, Tu chiz bari hai mast mast, Meri pant bhi sexy, Bholi bhali ladki, khol tere dil ki, pyar wali khidki* are songs that can be included in this category. Lewd songs, obscene pictures and violence are being exhibited everyday not only on the silver screen but on TV in our drawing rooms and every homes. Hooked on to such entertainment, the future generation is developing under such influence losing our culture and important values. It may be interesting to know that once film songs were banned from being broadcast at the early stage of our independence under the orders of the then Broadcasting and Informations Minister Shri B.V. Keskar because it eroded familial values and public morality. The film song, at that time, did not go beyond *Tu mera chand, main teri chandani* and *Chhor do anchal, jamana kya kahega*. Unfortunately today, Mahesh Bhatt, a film maker and Chairman of the Film and Television Institute of India under the same Ministry turns out future denizens of the celluloid and video world and says that watching pornographic films is a man's birthright. Therefore, there is nothing wrong in producing, exhibiting and viewing pronographic films.[8]

5.07 Scenes in Films

If every production and exhibition becomes art piece and then what is not art will be difficult to define. Such fine art, when imitated, would lead to lust and crime. It may be remembered that a man who stole a precious artefact from the National Museum, did so after getting a clue from seeing such a film. In the more recent Auto Shanker sex and multiple murder case, as per the defense Counsel's statement, the prime accused had seen films depicting sex, violence and illicit business and was thus misguided and ended up as a criminal. It was in the course of the judgement in the case that the Hon'ble Judges of the Apex Court posed certain question in the following words.[8]

> Whether it is compulsory that a heroine should invariably appear on the screen with accentuated angularities, deepened depressions and exaggerated protuberances of the body. It is an irrevocable convention that the violence unleashed by the wicked or the evil minded villain, or that the hero's valour in punishing those wicked and diabolic manner. . . exhibiting scenes of violence, sex, rape, boot-legging and drug trafficking, etc. in such a manner as to disturb or corrupt the minds of some viewers like children and particularly of those who are weak-minded, wayward, indiscplined, frustrated and like-

wise, who are very likely to become wicked and evil-minded and ultimately end up as criminals in organised crimes.

The Hon'ble Judges further hoped that all those concerned, in whose wisdom we have faith, will act promptly to set right this scenario. However, nothing has happened in these three years after the judgement and those, concerned with it, have opened the flood-gates and forfeited the people's faith in their wisdom. There is little hope on the horizon, for the the new mileu or globalisation, it is the pecuniary and cultural carpet beggars who rule the roost.[8]

5.08 Television

Films were problems enough but at least they are governed by a Censor Board and a cinema hall is physically an external phenomena and requires pre-planning for its viewing. A television, however, is an internal affair and simply requires switching on provided the electric supply is not erratic. The proliferation of private and foreign networks provide almost 18 hours of entertainment. For working couples, television is a cheap form of entertainment and serves as a baby-sitter.[9] However, TV needs a thorough policing and certain programmes and shows need to be banned or at least improved, otherwise the society is heading towards cultural doom. The poor quality of TV programme and showing of consumption of liquor at the slightest pretext is adversely affecting the population leading to increase in crime. In the name of freedom and modernity, the parents do not disallow their children from seeing TV and watching senseless violence, crimes and brutalitity and use of alcohol by the so-called respectable persons of the society. The beauty contests and fashion shows, frequently being shown on the small screen make young girls believe that mental capability has no place in comparison to the shapely figures with the result that some of girls have beginning to care more for the figures than to the development of mental capability or academic excellence. It is the beauty contestants who are blown out of proportion through TV, consequently like-minded girls have started attaching more importance to beauty and figures than anything else. If young girls are ready to be paraded before an audience in semi-nude dress, let that be done but why show them on T.V. Such exhibition on the small screen should be banned.[10]

5.09 Cable Television

New channels and newer programmes are bringing in more scenes of gore and flesh into the drawing room but that is being disturbed by the news that there are programmes on that day which are to be taken or seen at the late night.

In a report submitted to the Delhi High Court, the Central Board of Film Certification found that 705 programmes out of 3703, monitored during two months were not found O.K.[11]

The Board members have come down heavily on the lack of control over the programmes. They have expressed objection to the films with scenes of nudity being shown on TV. The argument is that though the movie has been cleared by the Censor Board for the big screen, they are not to be shown on small screen in drawing room, where the criteria is different. The Programme Code as per the Cable Television Network (Regulation) Act, 1995 is as under:[11]

I. No programme should be carried in the cable service which,

(a) offends against the good taste or decency;
(b) contains criticism of friendly countries;
(c) contains attack on religious or communities or visuals or words contemptuous of religious groups or which promote communal attitudes;
(d) contains anything obscene, defamatory, deliberate, false and suggestive innuendoes and half truth;
(e) is likely to encourage or incite violence or contains anything against maintenance of law and order or which promote anti-national attitudes;
(f) contains anything amounting to contempt of court;
(g) contains aspersions against the integrity of the President and Judiciary;
(h) contains anything affecting the integrity of the nation;
(i) criticises, maligns or slanders any individual in person or certain groups, segments of social, public and moral of the country;
(j) encourages superstitions or blind belief;
(k) denigrates women through the depiction in any manner of the figure of a woman, her form or body or any part thereof in such a way as to have the effect of being indecent, or derogatory to women, or is likely to deprive, corrupt or injure the public morality or morale;

(l) denigrates children;

(m) contains visuals or words which reflect a slandering, ironical and snobbish attitude in the portrayal of certain ethnic, linguistic and regional groups.

II. The Cable Operator should strive to carry programmes in his cable service which project women in a positive, leadership, role of sobriety, moral and character building qualities.

III. Programmes meant for Adults should normally be carried in the cable service after 11 P.M. and before 6 A.M.

IV. Care should be taken to ensure that programmes meant for children do not contain any bad language or explicit scenes of violence.

V. Programmes unsuitable for children must not be carried in the cable service at times when the largest number of children are viewing.

In the light of the criteria laid down by the Programme Code, the Board members made specific reference to some movies which had scenes of nudity. 'Carry on camping' was one such movie. 'Don't Look Now' was not considered appropriate by one member for viewing as the same was likely to have adverse impact on children's tender mind and should not, therefore, be shown during prime time. Movie 'Off and Running' had vulgar language and obscene scenes 'Big Steel' showed bare-breasted girls working for a hotel-bar, topless dancers and love-making in a car accompanied by a vulgar background sound.

The Board members even found dialogues with double meaning and vulgar. A scene from 'Doctor in Clover' in which a nurse is applying powder on a patient lying covered with a bed-sheet and upon which the patient tells the nurse that she was pulling the wrong thing. It was his thumb.

The Boards real objection has been to teleserials, both Indian and foreign. The Board members categorised those which should not be shown on TV. Some were approved with cuts and were meant to be shown at late nights presumably when the children would be asleep. The Board members further expressed objections to the programmes depicting excessive violence or glorification of criminals. The 'Horror Show, teleserial 'Aghori' were deemed unfit to be shown to the children. These programmes either should not be shown at all and if shown should be done at late nights. 'Tara' is another programme which the Board members felt should be either taken off or shown with cuts.[11]

In view of the Programme Codes for Cable TV, hardly any modern film, would be included in the category of being exhibited for the children.

5.10 Parents/Guardians Vigilance

Eminent educationists have recently pointed out at a conference organised by the Council of Board of School Education and the National Council of Education Research and Training (NCERT) that a child, by the time he attains the age of 18 years has witnessed on the television 30,000 murders and other programmes depicting violence and vulgarity thus doing away with the good done by education.[12] In this hasty interactive world of fast foods, a multitude of TV channels and fast sex, our children are missing out on the simple things of life. A child's activity-level certainly affects his development indirectly and of course, the way he is handled by others. A mother, for instance, may punish the active child, while an energetic father may show impatience towards a placid one, since he identifies closely with one similar to his own personalities. This, in many cases, could show the seed of an inferiority complex, where the child's self worth is under siege.[13]

As a rule, we people prefer to shift responsibility to the Government and blame the Government for everything that is happening against our interest. However, if audiences stayed away from halls, the films enter homes via television. The opening up of the air waves has led to fierce competition for audience ratings. Given the voracious appetite of television for software, what could be simpler than turning to films and programmes, based on films with song picturisations in the forefront. Since almost no songs are free of sexual innuendo at the least and explicit body gyrations at the most this violation of the sanctity at the home where parents normally held sway has finally stirred protest on a mass scale.[14]

However things cannot improve through holding of seminars, lodging of protests and holding strike. In the first instance, intellectual meet, intellectual discuss and intellectuals depart and the situation continue to deteriorate. When protest is lodged, the Minister or the top bureaucrat will listen, the official will note and nothing beyond this shall normally move. When strikes are resorted to, the Members of Parliament would discuss the matter of the deteriorating level of films and their harmful effects on society, particularly on children and adolescents. The film producers would point to the difficulties in the face of the escalating costs of making a film, crippling taxation, the steadily declining state of the theatres where the films were shown and the matter will remain unsettled.

The only way, therefore, could be the involvement of the parents with the children. The children want to talk to the parents and discuss their problems with them. The parents will have to spare some time for the children on a routine basis and better still would be to get him inducted to some lessons in music, either vocal or instrumental so that his appetite for cultural activity is satisfied and energy diverted to some useful work. Once a child has picked up any branch of classical music, all that happen in films and film music will appear to be insignificant for him. The author (K.K.) is asserting this on the basis of his personal experience which he had experimented with his own son who was inducted to learn playing of *tabla* and he lost all interest in the films of today. He tried to attain competency in music lessons.

The parents will also have to give up their own indulgence in TV films or video casettes. They are also required to give up smoking and drinking habits. The whole idea is to set an example before the child and divert his energies to some useful work.

REFERENCES

1. H.T. Correspondent (Calcutta), "Juvenile Delinquents get Death Sentence", *The Hindustan Times,* (Delhi Edn.) dated January 11, 1996.
2. Rohit Inder Singh, "The Legacy of Blood", *The Hindustan Times,* (Delhi Edn.) dated June 17, 1995.
3. The Hindustan Times (Correspondent)—New Delhi, "Priyadarshini Killer put in C.B.I. custody", *The Hindustan Times,* dated February 1, 1996.
4. Dr. Prabha Rani, "Video Sanskriti ke Changul Mein Bhavi Peerhee (English Translation—Future generation under the grip of Video Culture), *Hindustan (Hindi) (Patna* Edn.*) dated Sunday the 10th December 1995.*
5. Aruna Vasudeva, "Cinema altering the Statusquo convenient Scapegoat", *Sunday Magazine, The Hindustan Times,* (Delhi Edn.) dated July 23, 1995.
6. Himanshu Sekhar Jha, "Ban Adult Films", *The Hindustan Times* (Delhi Edn.) dated the 11th November 1995

7. Section 292 to Section 294 with State Amendments read as under:

292. Sale, etc., of obscene books, etc.:

(1) For the purpose of sub-section (2), book pamphlet, paper, writing, drawing, painting, representation, figure or any other object, shall be deemed to be obscene if it is lascivious or appeals to the prurient interest or if its effect, or (where it comprises two or more distinct items) the effect of any one of its items, is, if taken as a whole, such as to tend to deprave and corrupt persons who are likely, having regard to all relevant circumstances, to read, see or hear the matter contained or embodied in it.

(2) Whoever:

(a) sells, lets to hire, distributes, publicly exhibits or in any manner puts into circulation, or for purpose of sale, hire, distribution, public exhibition or circulation, makes, produces or has in possession any obscene book, pamphlet, paper, drawing, painting, representation or figure or any other obscene object whatever, or

(b) imports, exports or conveys any obscene object for any of the purposes aforesaid, or knowing or having reason to believe that such object will be sold, let to hire, distributed or publicly exhibited or in any manner put into circulation, or

(c) takes part in or receives profits from any business in the course of which he knows or has reasons to believe that any such obscene objects are, for any of the purposes aforesaid, made, produced, purchased, kept, imported, exported, conveyed, publicly exhibited or in any manner put into circulation, or

(d) advertises or makes known by any means, whatsoever, that any person is engaged or is ready to engage in any act which is an offence under this Section, or that any such obscene object can be procured from or through any person, or

(e) offers or attempts to do any act which is an offence under this section,

shall be punished on first conviction with imprisonment of either description for a term which may extend to two years, and with fine which may extend to two thousand rupees, and, in the event of a second or subsequent conviction, with imprisonment of either description for a term which may extend to five years, and also with fine which may extend to five thousand rupees.

Exception: This Section does not extend to:

(a) any book, pamphlet, paper, writing, drawing, painting, representation or figure:

(i) the publication of which is proved to be justified as being for the public good on the ground that such book, pamphlet, paper, writing, drawing, painting, representation or figure is in the interest of science, literature, art or learning or other objects of general concern, or

(ii) which is kept or used bona fide for religious purposes:

(b) any representation sculptured, engraved, painted or otherwise represented on or in:

(i) any ancient monument within the meaning of the Ancient Monuments and Archaeological Sites and Remains Act, 1958 (24) of 1958), or

(ii) any temple, or on any car used for the conveyance of idols, or kept or used for any religious purpose.

Local Amendments

ORISSA: Amended by Orissa Act 13 of 1962 [same as that of Tamil Nadu].

TAMIL NADU: [Amended by Tamil Nadu Act 25 of 1960.] In its application to the whole of the State of Tamil Nadu, in Section 292 the words "shall be punished with imprisonment of either description for a term which may extend to three months or with fine or with both" substitute the following, namely:

> "shall be punished with imprisonment of either description for a term which may extend to two years or with fine or with both:
> Provided that for a second or any subsequent offence under this section, he shall be punished with imprisonment of either description for a term which shall not be less than six months and not more than two years and with fine."

Local Amendments

Section 292-A:

ORISSA: Amended by Orissa Act 13 of 1962 [same as that of Tamil Nadu].

Tamil Nadu: [Amended by Tamil Nadu Act 25 of 1960.]

In its application to the whole of the State of Tamil Nadu, after Section 292 insert the following new Section namely,

"292-A" Printing etc. of grossly indecent or scurrilous matter or matter intended for blackmail.

Whoever

(a) prints or causes to be printed in any newspaper, periodical or circular, or exhibits or causes to be exhibited, to public view or distributes or causes to be distributed or in any manner puts into circulation any picture or any printed or written document which is grossly indecent, or is scurrilous or intended for blackmail, or

(b) sells or lets for hire, or for purpose of sale or hire makes, produces or has in his possession, any picture or any printed or written document which is grossly indecent or is scurrilous or intended for blackmail, or

(c) conveys any picture or any printed or written document which is grossly indecent or is scurrilous or intended for blackmail knowing or having reason to believe that such picture or document will be printed, sold, let for hire, distributed or publicly exhibited or in any manner put into circulation, or

(d) takes part in, or receives profits from, any business in the course of which he knows or has reason to believe that any such newspaper, periodical, circular, picture or other printed or written document is printed, exhibited, distributed, circulated, sold, let for hire, made, produced, kept, conveyed or purchased, or

(e) advertises or makes known by means whatsoever that any person is engaged or is ready to engage in any act which is an offence under this Section, or that any such newspaper, periodical, circular, picture or other printed or written document which is grossly indecent or is scurrilous or intended for blackmail can be procured from or through any person, or

(f) offers or attempts to do any act which is an offence under this Section, shall be punished with imprisonment of either description for a term which may extend to two years, or with fine, or with both.

Provided that for a second or any subsequent offence under this Section, he shall be punished with imprisonment of either description for a term which shall not be less than six months and not more that two years and with fine.

Explanation I: For the purpose of this section, the word 'scurrilous' shall be deemed to include any matter which is likely to be injurious to morality or is calculated to injure any person.

Provided that it is not scurrilous to express in good faith anything whatever respecting the conduct of:

(i) a public servant in the discharge of his public functions or respecting his character so far as his character appears in that conduct and no further; or

(ii) any person touching any public question, and respecting his character, so far as his character appears in that conduct and no further.

Explanation II: In deciding whether any person has committed an offence under this Section, the court shall have regard, *inter alia*, to the following considerations:

(a) the general character of the person charged, and where relevant, the nature of his business;

(b) the general character and dominant effect of the matter alleged to be grossly indecent or scurrilous or intended for blackmail;

(c) any evidence offered or called by or on behalf of the accused person as to his intention in committing any of the acts specified in this Section.

293. Sale, etc., of obscene objects to young person:

Whoever sells, lets to hire, distributes, exhibits or circulates to any person under the age of twenty years any such obscene object as it is referred to in the last preceding Section, or offers or attempts so to do, shall be punished.

On first conviction with imprisonment of either description for a term which may extend to three years, and with fine which may extend to two thousand rupees, and, in the event of a second or subsequent conviction, with imprisonment of either description for a term which may extend to seven years, and also with fine which may extend to five thousand rupees.

Local Amendments

ORISSA: Amended by Orissa Act 13 of 1962 (same as that of Tamil Nadu Act.)

TAMIL NADU: Amended by Tamil Nadu Act 25 of 1960. In its application to the whole of the state of Tamil Nadu in Section 293:

(a) for the words "any such obscene object as is referred to in the last preceding section" substitute the words, figures and letter, "any such obscene object is as reffered to in Section 292 or any such newspaper, periodical, circular, picture or other printed or written document as is referred to in Section 292-A."

(b) for the words " which may extend to six months" substitute the words "which may extend to three years."

(c) in the marginal note, after the words "obscene objects" insert the words "and grossly indecent or scurrilous matter intended for blackmail."

294. Obscene acts and songs:

Whoever, to the annoyance of other,

(a) does any obscene act in any public place; or

(b) sings, recites or utters any obscene songs, ballad or words, in or near any public place.

shall be punished with imprisonment of either description for a term which may extend to three months, or with fine, or with both.

8. Sumer Kaul, "Culture of Carpet baggers", *The Hindustan Times,* (Delhi Edn.) dated Jan. 24, 1996.
9. Ashok Malik, "Is Television Guilty", *Sunday Hindustan Times,* (Delhi Edn.), dated July 23, 1995.
10. Seema Khanna, (Letters) "Ill Effects of TV", *The Hindusatan Times* (Delhi Edn.), dated January 31, 1996.
11. Wilson John, "Cheap Show", *The Hindustan Times,* (Delhi Edn.) (Metropolitan) dated January 31, 1996.
12. S. Shridhar (Letters), "Spate of Vulgar Films", *The Hindustan Times,* (Delhi Edn.) dated January 24, 1996.
13. Neelam Mathews, "Are we Rearing Brats?" *Saturday Times, Times of India,* (Delhi Edn.) dated February 3, 1996.

Chapter VI

CHILD LABOUR

6.01 Introduction

Article 24 of the Constitution of India, prohibits the employment of children below the age of 14 years to work in any factory or mine or engaged in any hazardous employment. Section 2 (II) of The Child Labour (Prohibition and Regulation) Act, 1986 (No. 61 of 1986) defines child as meaning a person who has not completed his 14th year of age. According to Section 2 (c) of The Factories Act, 1948, (Act no. 63 of 1948), "Child" means a person who has not completed his 15th year of age.

In case of omission, the onus to prove that the person is not under such age is on the accused.[1]

6.02 Hazardous Process[2]

"Hazardous Process" means any process or activity in relation to an industry specified in the First Schedule[3] where, unless special care is taken, raw materials, used therein or the intermediate or finished products, by-products, wastes of effluents thereof would

(i) cause material impairment to the health of the persons engaged in or connected therewith, or
(ii) result in the pollution of the general environment.

Provided that the State Government may, by notification in the official Gazette, amend the First Schedule by way of addition, omission or variation of any industry specified in the said Schedule.

6.03 Prohibition of Employment of Children—Statutory Provisions

I. No child shall be employed or permitted to work in any of the occupation set forth in Part I of the Schedule or in any workshop wherein any of the processes set forth in Part B of the Schedule is carried out provided that nothing in this Section shall apply to any workshop wherein any process is carried out by the occupier of his family or to any school established by, or receiving assistance or recognition from Government.[4]

THE SCHEDULE
(See Section 3)

Part A
OCCUPATION

Any occupation connected with

(1) Transport of passengers, goods or mails by railways;
(2) Cinder picking, cleaning of ash pit or building operation in the railway premises;
(3) Work in a catering establishment at a railway station, involving the movement of a vendor or any other employee of the establishment from one platform to another or into or out of a moving train;
(4) Work relating to the construction of a railway station or with any other work where such work is done in close proximity to or between the railway lines;
(5) A port authority within the limits of any port.

Part B
PROCESSES

(1) Bidi-making
(2) Carpet weaving
(3) Cement manufacture, including bagging of cement
(4) Cloth printing, dyeing
(5) Manufacture of matches, explosives and fire works
(6) Mica cutting and Splitting
(7) Shellac manufacture
(8) Soap manufacture

(9) Tanning
(10) Wool-cleaning
(11) Building and Construction Industry

II. *Secs. 67 & 27 of the Factories Act Prohibits the employment of women and children in factories.*

The two Sections are as under:

"*67. Prohibition of employment of young children*: No child who has not completed his fourteenth year shall be required or allowed to work in any factory".

"*27. Prohibition of employment of children near cotton openers*: No woman or child shall be employed in any part of a factory for pressing cotton in which a cotton-opener is at work:

Provided that if the feed-end of a cotton-opener is in a room separated from the delivery end of a partition extending to the roof or to such height as the Inspector may in any particular case specify in writing, women and children may be employed on the side of the partition where the feed-end is situated."

6.04 Other Provisions Controling the Employment of Children

Sections 68–75 of The Factories Act, 1948, embodies the regulations controlling the employment of children in industrial employment. These Sections are reproduced below:

"*68: Non-adult workers to carry tokens:* A child who has completed his fourteenth year or an adolescent[5] shall not be required or allowed to work in any factory unless

(a) a certificate of fitness granted with reference to his under Section 69 is in the custody of the manager of the factory, and
(b) such child or adolescent carries while he is at work a token giving a reference to such certificate."

"*69. Certificate of fitness:* (1) A certifying surgeon shall, on the application of any young person or his parent or guardian accompanied by a document signed by the Manager of a factory that such person will be employed therein if certified to be fit for work in a factory, or on the application of the manager of the factory in which any young person wishes to work, examine such person and ascertain his fitness for work in a factory.

(2) The certifying surgeon, after examination, may grant to such young person, in the prescribed form, or may renew

(a) a certificate of fitness to work in a factory as a child, if he is satisfied that the young person has completed his fourteenth year, that he has attained the prescribed physical standards and that he is fit for such work;

(a) a certificate of fitness to work in a factory as an adult, if he is satisfied that the young person has completed his fifteenth year, and is fit for a full day's work in a factory:

Provided that unless the certifying surgeon has personal knowledge of the place where the young person proposes to work and of the manufacturing process in which he will be employed, he shall not grant or renew a certificate under this sub-section until he has examined such place.

(3) A certificate of fitness granted or renewed under sub-section (2)

(a) shall be valid only for a period of twelve months from the date thereof;

(b) may be made subject to conditions in regard to the nature of the work in which the young person may be employed, or requiring re-examination of the young person before the expiry of the period of twelve months.

(4) A certifying surgeon shall revoke any certificate granted or renewed under sub-section (2), if in his opinion the holder of it is no longer fit to work in the capacity stated therein in a factory.

(5) Where a certifying surgeon refuses to grant or renew a certificate or a certificate of the kind requested or revokes a certificate, he shall, if so requested by any person who could have applied for the certificate or the renewal thereof, state his reason in writing for so doing.

(6) Where a certificate under this Section with reference to any young person is granted or renewed subject to such conditions as are referred to in Clause (b) of sub-section (3), the young person shall not be required or allowed to work in any factory except in accordance with those conditions.

(7) Any fee payable for a certificate under this Section shall be paid by the occupier and shall not be recoverable from the young person, his parents or guardian."

"70. *Effect of certificate of fitness granted to adolescent:* (1) An adolescent who has been granted a certificate of fitness to work in a factory as an adult under Clause (b) of sub-section (2) of Section 69, and while at work in a factory carries a token giving reference to the certificate, shall be deemed to be an adult for all the purposes of Chapters VI and VIII.

(1-A) No female adolescent or a male adolescent who has not attained the age of seventeen years but who has been granted a certificate of fitness to work in a factory as an adult shall be required or allowed to work in any factory except between 6 A.M. and 7 P.M.;

Provided that the State Government may, by notification in the official Gazette, in respect of any factory or group or class or description of factories:

(i) vary the limits laid down in this sub-section so, however, that no such Section shall authorise the employment of any female adolescent between 10 P.M. and 5 A.M.;
(ii) grant exemption from the provisions of this sub-section in case of serious emergency where national interest is involved.

(2) An adolescent who has not been granted a certificate of fitness to work in a factory as an adult under the aforesaid Clause (b) shall, notwithstanding his age, be deemed to be a child for the purposes of this Act."

"71. *Working hours for children:* (1) No child shall be employed or permitted to work, in any factory

(a) for more than four hours in any day
(b) during the night

Explanation: For the purposes of this sub-section *'night'* shall mean a period of at lease twelve consecutive hours which include the interval between 10 P.M. and 6 A.M.

(2) The period of work of all children employed in a factory shall be limited to two shifts which shall not overlap or spread over more than five hours each; and each child shall be employed in only one of the relays which shall not, except with the previous permission in writing of the Chief Inspector, be changed more frequently than once in a period of thirty days.

(3) The provisions of Section 52 shall apply also to child workers and no exemption from the provisions of that Section may be granted in respect of any child.

(4) No child shall be required or allowed to work in any factory on any day on which he has already been working in another factory.

(5) No female child shall be required or allowed to work in any factory except between 8 A.M. and 7 P.M."

"72. *Notice of periods of work for children:* (1) These shall be displayed and correctly maintained in every factory in which children are employed, in accordance with the provisions of sub-section (2) of Section 108,[6] a notice of periods of work for children, showing clearly for every day the periods during which children may be required or allowed to work.

(2) The periods shown in the notice required by Sub-section (1) shall be fixed beforehand in accordance with the method laid down for adult workers in Section 61, and shall be such that children working for those periods would not be working in contravention of any of the provisions of Section 71.

(3) The provisions of sub-sections (8), (9) and (10) of Section 61 shall apply also to the notice required by sub-section (1) of this Section."

"73. *Register of child workers:* (1) The manager of every factory in which children are employed shall maintain a register of child workers, to be available to the Inspector at all times during working hours or when any work is being carried on in a factory, showing-

(a) the name of each child worker in the factory,
(b) the nature of his work,
(c) the group, if any, in which he is included,
(d) where his group works on shifts, the relay to which he is allotted, and
(e) The number of his certificate of fitness granted under Section 69.

(1-A) No child worker shall be required or allowed to work in any factory unless his name and other particulars have been entered in the register of child workers.

(2) State Government may prescribe the form of the register of child workers, the manner in which it shall be maintained and the period for which it shall be preserved."

"*74. Hours of work to correspond with notice under Section 72 and Register under Section 73:* No child shall be employed in any factory otherwise than in accordance with the notice of periods of work for children displayed in the factory and the entries made beforehand against his name in the register of child workers of the factory."

"*75. Power to require medical examination*: Where an Inspector is of opinion

(a) that any person working in a factory without a certificate of fitness is a young person, or
(b) that a young person working in a factory with a certificate of fitness is no longer fit to work in the capacity stated therein,

he may serve on the manager of the factory, a notice requiring that such person or young person, as the case may be, shall be examined by a certifying surgeon, and such person or young person shall not, if the Inspector so directs, be employed, or permitted to work, in any factory until he has been so examined and has been granted a certificate of fitness or a fresh certificate of fitness, as the case may be, under Section 69, or has been certified by the certifying surgeon examining him not to be a *young person.*"[7]

6.05 Gross Violation of Child's Rights in Industrial Employment

Though we have been talking of the evils of child labour for the past so many years and laws have been enacted to regulate the employment of children and the State have set up agencies to look into the problems of the employment of children, in such jobs as may prove hazardous and dangerous to their lives, yet the abolition of child labour is a distant dream. The child labour instead of decreasing is increasing primarily because child labour for quite a good number of families is compulsory for the survival of the family and the indifferent attitude of the enforcing agencies towards their problems. The result is that child labour instead of decreasing is increasing result being that the children continue to work in the most hazardous condition and compulsory education as enshrined in Article 45 of the Constitution is not being achieved.

The presence of child labour in hazardous industries is a gross violation of human rights. The children are made to face slow, as well as on the spot, deaths in industries like glass factories, cracker factories, brass-wares, lock, slate pencil, balloons, carpet industries, sari industries, brick kilns and other industries etc.

Cracker Factories

Explosion in cracker factories is not a new phenomenon and every year such accidents take place killing men, women and children to quote, for instance, blasts in Shivakashi in July, 1992 and September, 1993 took tolls of thirty and sixty lives respectively. In March 1994, four persons lost their lives in cracker factory near Bhubneswar, the capital city of Orissa. In May 1994, nearly a dozen persons were killed during an explosion in cracker factory in Ahmedabad. In October 1994, thirty persons were killed and twenty-four persons were injured in Jhansi cracker factory. Every year there are industrial accidents in Rohtak (Haryana). In 1995 in a ghastly accident in a Fire Cracker Factory at Rhotak, twenty-three persons (four males, thirteen females and six children) were burnt to death.[8]

Slate Factories

There is a Slate Pencil Factory at Mandsaur (M.P.), which employs children where, out of a total work force of 12,000 persons, nearly one thousand are children meaning thereby that the children constitute 8.33 per cent of the total work force. In the Slate industry at Markapur in A.P., out of a total work force of 15,000, child workers constitute about 25 per cent of the total work force, that is, their strength is 3750.[8]

The dust raised in the process of pencil cutting is inhaled by workers including children resulting in development in silicosis in lungs. This disease causes their early deaths. Ironically, the children who manufacture these pencils have no opportunity to use them inspite of so many literacy programmes in this country. Education at the primary level is a distant dream for these hapless children.[9]

Lock Industry

The Lock Industry at Aligarh (U.P) has a work force of eight to nine lakhs. The population of the child labour is between seven to ten thousands which accounts for 9 to 11 per cent of the total work force.[8]

Brass-ware Industry

Moradabad is known as Peetal Nagari because of a large number of brass-ware industries where children constitute nearly 27 to 30 per cent of the total work-force. Children in workshop have been found to stand bare-footed on top of the underground furnaces. In the process, the children put in the raw material and remove the molten brass which is placed in iron crucible with tongs. If the crucible slips, while removing it from the furnace there is always the risk of the child losing his feet. The adult worker manages to move away to a safe distance.[8]

Glass Industry

Ferozabad has a large number of bangle factories. The bangles are made beautifully from glass. Out of total work force of 2,00,000 (two lakhs) fifty thousand children work and constitute 25 per cent of the total work force. They are made to work in the most hazardous process of removing molten glass from the furnace. The furnace are designed to be operated by adult members. Thus while working on the furnace the children get nearly burnt. There are reports that when the children get seriously injured, in some cases they have been thrown into the furnace and finished off presumably to avoid payment of compensation and obviate legal complications.[8]

Match Industry

In match industry, the workers are required to handle highly explosive chemicals and working in a match factory is not free from the hazard.

Match industry is classified into four categories. These are:

Category	*Particulars*
A	Fully mechanised
B	Partially mechanised
C	Fully hand made in small sectors
D	Fully hand made in tiny sectors

The Government's policy leans towards the hand made sectors. The distinction between small sector and tiny sector is made on the basis of production capacity and some of the owners of match industries very often go on changing their category. A four member team of NHRC visited the State of Tamil Nadu in December, 1994 and the Commission's assessment is that there are 8000 and 22000 child workers in 'C' and 'D' categories respectively of match factories. These figures are, however, contested by various N.G.O.'s besides UNICEF who quote these figures as 15,000 and 50,000 in 'C' and 'D' categories respectively of Match Industries.

The condition of the child labour in Shivakashi Match Industry is very pitiable. Six to seven year children are driven out of their homes as early as 4 to 5 A.M. and they return at about 7 to 8 P.M. on buses, lorries and even tractors. In the child labour force, the girls outnumber boys. The girls are preferred over boys in the matter of employments since they are paid less for doing works for longer hours.[11]

Beedi Making

There is a prohibition of employment of children in any workshop wherein Beedi-making process is set forth but this provision of Section 3 of the Child Labour (Prohibition and Regulation) Act is inapplicable where the occupier of the family carries out the process.

In Beedi-making industry, workers are given a pass-book to get their quota of tobacco from the Central Excise Authorities. Most of these pass-books are in the name of husbands. While the wives and children sweat it out rolling beedis, the husband takes away the income as the wages are given only to the pass-book holders. Thus, the condition of the women and children in Beedi-making industry is a pitiable one.[10]

Carpet Industry

It is the Indian carpet industry that commands the choicest of coercive powers of Mirzapur-Bhadohi belt of U.P. and as such the incidence of child labour which crosses the figures of 60,000 becomes a major case of intrusion of human rights. The child sits in a dingy mud house from 7 A.M. to 5 P.M. with a break for an hour between 12 to 1, using his thin small fingers to create the weft and weave carpets that would be earning foreign exchange for the country.

In carpets of high quality, knotting the weft strings are drawn very closely and the weaver has to pierce the fingers through them in order to draw the woollen thread. Thin and supple fingers and the keen sight to scrutinise the design details on the graph is the most suitable requirement for the job. Since children possess these faculties on account of nature and tender age, it leads to the exploitation of labour easily available. As such there is a direct co-relation to the employment of child labour and incidence of production of carpet of high knottage. So, other than the natural ability, the greater the quality the higher the input of labour. Thus the relationship of the labour intensive and cost-effective ratio is amply visible.

As a matter of fact, export earnings in India in 1994–95 amounted to Rs. 1820 crores as compared to Rs. 1390 crores in 93–94 and 992 crores in 1992–93. So in the schemes of things, there are sixty thousand children on one hand and Rs. 1820 crores in foreign exchange. The supremacy and the clout of the exporters is well known. Poverty is the main cause of exploitation of child labour in carpet industry.[12]

Sari Industry

Banarasi Saris are the most aristocratic piece of garment for women in Indian conditions. The conditions of weaving and embellishing the Banarasi saris are such that the concentration of child labour in it is greater than that in the carpet industry. Incidentally, sari industry is not included in the list of industries involving hazardous process in the First Schedule of Section 2(cb) of the Factories Act. Still involvement of child labour in the industry is a thing which cannot be ignored. Prof. R.K. Mishra of Banaras University in his preliminary report records that the condition of child labour engaged in sari industry is quite deplorable. They are made to work from the age of five years. The boy of today from Ansari family and some boys among the Hindus start with no other future than to join the profession of their fathers, in the childhood and by the time they grow to be master weaver their eyes become weak and bad.[13] They are, thus, ruined.

6.06 Poverty, the Main Cause of Child Labour

Investigators and experts on child labour have ascribed the unfortunate situation of employment of children in hazardous processes to the economic compulsions of the parents and to the lack of will of the rulers in making education compulsory for the children at least up to the age of fourteen years.[12]

Although the Constitution has provided specific provisions for the children vide Art. 39(e) and (f) by promising them opportunities and facilities to develop in a healthy manner and in conditions of freedom and dignity and also the State's endeavour to provide this by the year 1960, they have remained a pipedream and observed in the breach of the mandate in Shivakshi and elsewhere in the country where the number of child labourers below the age of 14 is estimated at 1.36 crores.[11]

Child labour was found more economic because of low wages. The employees put forward the plea that its abolition would not only escalate the cost of production but would also add to the hardship to the people.[11]

In a survey conducted by Mode Research Private Ltd. in the Mirzapur Bhadohi region, the family income of the respondents showed low figure of 397 to 428 P.M. with an average of Rs 411 P.M. Low income and the inability to provide education to their children compel the parents to push their tender hands to work; lack of education and income become perpetual contributors to the child labour. Even among those enrolled, 96.7 per cent never attended and only 3.3 per cent ever attended school.[12]

Below are a few instances to show how poverty linked exploitation becomes a compulsion and a child becomes the victim of circumstances.

(1) A ten year boy narrated how his father took a loan of Rs. 1000 from a loom owner for buying a cow for providing

milk to his two sons and since the man would never be able to pay off the loan, the child must weave in lieu thereof. Ever since the school came up because of the efforts of NGO, CREDA, he attends school from 7–10 hrs in the morning and on return to home, he finds the loom owner waiting for him; if he resists, he is spun around with lashings and pushed in the direction of the loom where he must work till sun sets. His parents are unable to utter a word, because the debt has to be paid by the child.[12]

(2) A girl child in one of the schools in Varanasi told that she was in the school only to eat the food. She, otherwise was a loom worker.[12]

(3) Parveen (12) wanted to go to school unaware that death awaits her. Salim, her father, is counting days. Her mother is already dead. They were working in Slate Pencil Factory in Mandsaur and contracted silicosis, a terminal disease. She was one of the five children produced before the journalists by the Activists of Bachpan Bachao Andolan (BBA) at a Slate Factory Mandsaur at about the middle of May 1995.[9]

(4) Arif had to leave school to support the family after the death of his father from silicosis. He got the work in the same Slate Factory. He too has contracted the silicosis.[9]

(5) Seven year's Mange Lal was rarely paid. His employer told him that his wages are being adjusted against the loan of Rs. 8000 taken by his father. His mother died of silicosis and father is on death bed. He was called by the employer only the next day after he was rescued.[9]

6.07 Conclusion

Child labour is not a problem that touches only one sector. It has everything to do with education, health, social welfare and the infrastructure that deals with basic amenities like rural water supply and electricity. Electrification does not mean only raising of poles and giving connection to houses. Electrification, in true sense, means generation of power and regular supplies. For that we need competent, efficient and honest public servants and not the manner in which electricity is supplied in the present day scenario.

Social work and welfare involves a willingness to make sacrifices for the common cause. An economic cement would be more permanent than one of fear and insecurity. The important component of that cement must be solidarity of all people and their determination to defend the child's freedom, and child's childhood. The hard core of that solidarity must be an anti-corruptive mobilisation that works against the opulent rich.

Although the Child Labour (Protection and Regulation) Act was enacted in 1986, the enforcement rate is very low, rather negligibly low. No enactment of law would be effective unless its enforcement is done in right earnest. The Government and NGOs must make sincere efforts to eliminate this social evil and give what is due to the children, the national asset and the hope for the coming years. The basic requirement of a child is his childhood, nutrition, health, education and a bright future.

REFERENCES

1. Sec. 104 of Factories Act, 1948:

   Onus as to age: (1) When any act or omission would, if a person were under a certain age, be an offence punishable under this Act, and such person is in the opinion of the Court prima facie under such age, the burden shall be on accused to prove that such person is not under such age.

   (2) A declaration in writing by a certifying surgeon relating to a worker that he has personally examined him and believes him to be under the age stated in such declaration shall, for the purpose of this Act and the rules made thereunder, be admissible as evidence of the age of that worker.
2. Vide Section 2 (cb) of the Factories Act, 1948.
3. THE FIRST SCHEDULE OF FACTORIES ACT

   See Sec. (cb)

   Ins. by Act 20 of 1987, S. 45 (w.e.f. 1-2-1987)

   List of Industries Involving Hazardous Processes

   "1. Ferrous Metallurgical Industries
   - Integrated Iron and Steel
   - Ferro-alloys
   - Special Steels

   2. Non-ferrous Metallurgical Industries
   - Primary Metallurgical Industries, namely zinc, lead, copper, manganese and aluminum

   3. Foundries (Ferrous and non-ferrous)
   - Castings and forgings including cleaning or smoothening/roughening by sand and shot blasting

4. Coal (including Coke) industries
   — Coal, Lignite, Coke etc.
   — Fuel gases (including coal gas, producer gas, water gas)
5. Power Generating Industries
6. Pulp and Paper (including paper products) Industries
7. Fertilizer Industries
   — Nitrogenous
   — Phosphatic
   — Mixed
8. Cement Industries
   — Portland Cement (including slag cement, puzzolona cement and their products)
9. Petroleun Industries
   — Oil Refining
   — Lubricating Oils and Greases
10. Petro-chemical Industries
11. Drugs and Pharmaceuticals
12. Fermentation Industries (Distilleries and Breweries)
13. Rubber (Synthetic) Industries
14. Paints and Pigment Industries
15. Leather Tanning Industries
16. Electroplating Industries
17. Chemical Industries
    — Coke Oven By-products and Coal-tar Distillation products
    — Industrial Gases (nitrogen, oxygen, acetylene, argon, carbon-dioxide, nitrous-oxide, hydrogen, sulphur dioxide, halogenated hydrocarbon, ozone etc.)
    — Industrial Carbon
    — Alkalies and Acids
    — Chromates and di-chromates
    — Lead and its compounds
    — Electrochemicals (metallic sodium, potassium and magnesium, chlorates, perchlorates and peroxides)
    — Electrothermal products (artificial abrasive calcium carbide)
    — Nitrogenous compounds (cyanides, cyanamides and other nitrogenous compounds)
    — Phosphorous and its compounds
    — Halogens and Halogenated compounds (Chlorine, Fluorine, Bromine and Iodine)
    — Explosives (including Industrial explosives and detonators and fuses)
18. Insecticides, Fungicides, Herbicides and other Pesticides Industries
19. Synthetic Resin and Plastics
20. Man-made Fibre (Cellulosic and non-cellulosic) Industry
21. Manufacture and Repair of Electrical Accumulators
22. Glass and Ceramics
23. Grinding or Glazing of Metals
24. Manufacture, Handling and Processing of Asbestos and its Products
25. Extraction of Oils and Fats from Vegetable and Animal Sources

26. Manufacture, Handling and use of Benzene and Substances containing Benzene
27. Manufacture Process and Operations involving Carbon-disulphide
28. Dyes and Dye-stuff including their Intermediates
29. Highly Flammable Liquids and Gases

4. Vide Section 3 of the Child Labour (Prohibition and Regulation) Act, 1986.
5. According to Section 2 (b) of the Factories Act, 1948, "*adolescent*" means a person who has completed his fifteenth year of age but has not completed his eighteenth year.
6. Section 108 of "The Factories Act" reads as under:

   "*108. Display of notice*: (1) In addition to the notices required to be displayed in any factory by or under this Act, these shall be displayed in every factory, a notice containing such abstracts of this Act and of the rules made thereunder as may be prescribed and also the name and address of the Inspector and the certifying surgeon.

   (2) All notices required by or under this Act to be displayed in a factory shall be in English and in a language understood by the majority of the workers in the factory, and shall be displayed at some conspicuous and convenient place at or near the main entrance to the factory and shall be maintained in a clean and legible condition.

   (3) The Chief Inspector may, by order in writing served on the manager of any factory, require that these shall be displayed in the factory, any other notice or poster relating to the health, safety or welfare of the workers in the factory."
7. Section 2 (d) of "The Factories Act, 1948" defines "*young person*" as meaning a person who is either a child or an adolescent."
8. A report by Neera Burra, "Playing with Fire", *The Hindustan Times*, (Delhi Edn.) dated June 4, 1995.
9. News item by a Staff Reporter, "Death comes written on a slate", *Times of India* (Delhi Edn.) dated May 24, 1995.
10. Madhusudan Sahoo, "Taking their Childhood away", *The Hindustan Times*, (Delhi Edn.) dated June 15, 1995.
11. From C.S. Jayarama, "Tender Years turned to Ashes", *The Hindustan Times*, (Delhi Edn.) dated June 15, 1995.
12. A Report by Uma Nair, "To work is to live", *The Hindustan Times*, dated 18.7.1995.
13. Chanchal Sarkar, "Bonded from Birth", *The Hindustan Times*, (Delhi Edn.) dated July 5, 1995.

Chapter VII

CHILD ABUSE

7.01 Introduction

Article 23 of the Constitution guarantees prohibition of traffic in human beings and also provides for punishment in accordance with law for any contravention of the provisions.

Inspite of the mandate to the people enshrined in the Constitution and the penal provisions vide Sections 363A, 366, 366A, 366B, 372, 373, 374, Clause sixthly, 376 and 377 of the Indian Penal Code,[1] Child prostitution exists in India as well all over South Asia. According to a study conducted by International Labour Organisation (ILO) in the year 1994, Thailand tops the list having more than six lakhs child prostitutes, India about four lakhs and Phillipines has about sixty thousand. Even boys are not spared. Sri Lanka has about forty thousand boy prostitutes below the age of sixteen years, sought for both by pervert men as well as by playful women.[2]

According to the President of *'Patita Uddhar Samity'* about 30% of the prostitutes are children. The report of the Social Advisory Committee states that the number of prostitutes in six major cities of the country is between one to two lakhs. It adds that 20 per cent of them are children below the age of 15 years.[2]

In India child prostitution stems from child labour. As per off record estimates, of the Indian Council of Child Welfare (ICWA) it appears that there are one crore child wage earners all over the country. Majority of them have been forced into prostitution wing to poverty and utter destitution. Rural poverty and pressing socio-economic conditions have served to expand the potential supply of child prostitutes. Even parents, on account of utter destitution have knowingly offered the child into the clutches of sex traffickers. Besides economic stress, other causes are kidnapping of minor girls, social customs and tradition in some communities, particularly in the areas bordering the States of Madhya Pradesh, Gujarat and Rajasthan, the parents have willingly pushed the girl child to the profession of prostitution. Even brothel-keepers have a number of agents who are on the look out for such innocent children.[2]

The sexual exploitation of a child on a commercial scale is simply a reduction of the human being to an object for the use of a more powerful person. A child is not a consenting party in any such activity. Sexual acts can easily damage a child's small or immature body and make him vulnerable to sexually transmitted diseases. Perpetration of violence from customers, pimps or madams is a regular feature of the lives of many child prostitutes. Physical health of such victims are aggravated by lack of medical care. Children inducted into the sex activities frequently experience guilt and low self-esteem. Many of them attempt to avoid or escape their families.[3]

Owing to poverty, a number of minor girls start as domestic help. These minor girls are employed on a paltry amount of 100 to 200 rupees per month. Their hours of work are not fixed. They are often raped by their unscrupulous employers and on account of incidents of repeated acts of rape, they become prostitutes. At times the mother of prostitute herself initiates the daughter to the flesh trade as she is devoid of any source of living and finds no alternative future for the girl.[2]

7.02 The South-East Scenario

The brisk business of child prostitution in Thailand and other South-East Asian countries started in the year 1967. The U.S. Government, occupied with Vietnam war had signed an agreement with Thailand for enabling the U.S. soldiers to come ashore for rest and recreation, thus providing an international legal sanction to the illegal flesh trade.

A member of the N.Y. Branch of the International Campaign to 'End Child Prostitution in Asian Tourism' (ECPAT) states that the flesh trade in South-East Asian region thrives in Thailand, Sri Lanka and Phillipines by leaps and bounds A survey by ECPAT revealed that 6000 to 8000 Nepalese girls between the ages of

10–14 years are being traded across the border in India. Most of these Nepalese and other similar girls are enticed in a cladestine manner are brought to metropolitan cities of the country, where unwilling and resistent girls are subjected to inhuman conditions including rape, starvation, assaults etc. as a conditioning measure and to punish them for expressing against willingness. Having no other means by which they can be rescued they give up and submit. The provisions of Sections 372, 373, 366A and 366B have no meaning for these hapless girl for want of vigilance and proper enforcement.

In the premier tourist spots of Sri Lanka, young boys earn their livelihood through sex trade. Paedophiles operate sex syndicates in the smaller hotels and the ambiguous laws invariably hold the child guilty. The Government of Sri Lanka is conscious of it and asserts that it is fully committed to redress the gross violation of child rights. The Hon'ble Minister of Social Welfare referring to the Convention on Children's Rights said that his country ratified in 1991, and which made a special mention of the child abuse admits that the situation is horrifying and the long term and the lasting solution have to be found and it is the adults and not the children who are real culprit. The Government has to change attitudes, take the media into confidence, take the law enforcement agencies efficient and effective and pave the way for responsible tourism.[4]

7.03 Efforts by the ECPAT (End Child Prostitution in Asian Tourism)

The concept that children are the country's greatest resource and to destroy them means to play with the destiny of the nation, and children deserve to be treated with respect and love led to the establishment of ECPAT which at present functions through more than 250 groups in coalition with over twenty-five countries world-wide. The committees in each country raise public awareness and promote legal applications.

The International Office in Bangkok, maintains its co-ordinating and monitoring role and looking forward to extend the campaign beyond Asia and take up other problems beyond tourism. The ECPAT during the year 1994 continued to work closely with Interpol and with several national police forces to seek ways and means to bring to trial those guys who sexually abuse children. In some cases children who have worked in brothels have also been released and have been assisted by ECPAT group through rehabilitation programmes.[3]

V.N. Kakar[5] recalls his days of 1946 when he was a Post-Graduate student of Islamia College, Peshawar. He, alongwith two or three class mates chanced to see in Green Hotel of Peshawar, a get-together of Pathan political leaders. The leaders had assembled there and they were taking tea with roasted chicken as snacks and behind the chair of every leader stood a tender boy. These boys were known as *'NADAS'* who were supposed to cater to the sexual needs of the master. These *nadas* were not the preserve of political leader's only but almost every person who mattered kept *'nadas'* who constituted part and parcel of general environment of sodomy. While it is endemic in N.W.F.P., it is widespread in Baluchistan. No survey or research have known to have been conducted on these boys who are the victims of unnatural offences and made to serve as fodder for the unscrupulous depraved adults.

7.04 Incest

Incest is a sexual relationship between persons so closely related that marriage between them is not permitted. In other words, it is a sexual abuse within the family. The tragic element in this type of depraved act is that the abused child, overwhelmed by unfamiliar sensations by the strength of the abuser feels so terribly let down, that the life period is coloured by the violations.

7.05 Side Effects of Child Abuse

A child who is born, is thrust into an unfamiliar world, is left at the mercy of adults. A responsible and sensible adult may be loving and caring but where the adult is insensitive, the child might become object of abuses, humiliation, cruelty, molestation etc. The infantile dependence gives the child to touch the responsive chords of adults, who more often take delight in caring for him. When this takes place, the child develops the capacity to trust, an ability that is absolutely essential for his inner growth and for becoming an emotionally mature individual. A child is under a profound belief that he won't be let down by those in whom he has trust and faith. If, contrary to his belief, he is hurt by an adult, he loses the basic trust, which immediately changes the way wherein suspicion, fear and a basic distrust are his favourite companion. The absence of trust can develop into infantile schizophrenia. A person, who cannot trust lacks spontaneity, tends to look on the gloomy side and hesitate to move forward. The abused tend to harbour a sense of being unclean and defiled and this continues even long after the actual event and this tendency is reflected in obsessive cleanliness and intolerance of anything having link with the feeling of dirt inside him.[6]

7.06 Judicial Evaluation of Offence of Child Rape

There is no separate rape laws for the act of sexual assaults on a child, except that according to clause sixthly of Section 375 I.P.C., sexual act with a female under sixteen years of age even with consent amounts to rape. As a matter of fact, if rape is committed on a child, who obviously is not in a position to offer any substantial resistance, the mandatory sentence could be life transportation and if the act of sexual assault is followed with a murder the mandatory sentence could be death sentence. In such a case death sentence should be a rule and life transportation an exception in very rare cases for reasons to be recorded in the Court's order. In the well proved case of rape with murder of Guria, a six year child by the accused, who took the child to the sugar-cane field satisfied his lust and committed her murder, the trial Court awarded death sentence but the sentence was modified to life imprisonment by the High Court.[7] In *Satyaveer* v. *State of Rajasthan*,[8] the accused had committed rape on a girl child aged nine years, the trial Court had awarded the extreme sentence provided under the law. The High Court, while holding that punishment should fit the crime and a lenient punishment in a grave crime is a serious distortion since that finds no impact on the pan on the criminal, and undue sympathy would harm the cause of justice and would undermine the efficacy of law but looking to the age of the accused, which was twenties at the time of commission of crime, the sentence was modified to R.I. for ten years with a fine of Rs. one hundred. Where two accused persons Raju and Pappu committed rape of a girl twelve years of age but F.I.R. was lodged after one month of the commission of the offence, the Trial Court as well as the High Court accepted the explanation given before the Court for the delay and dismissed the appeal against the sentence holding that in a case of this type, no leniency can be shown to the accused.[9] In *Madan Gopal Kakkad* v. *Naval Dubey,*[10] where the accused a doctor, conversant with the anatomy and medical science caused slight penetration into the private part of a girl aged 9 years not to substantially hurt her, was convicted by the Supreme Court holding that a conviction can be sustained even if there is no corroboration in the deposition of a prosecutrix provided the evidence of the victim does not suffer from any basic infirmity and the probability factor does not render it unworthy of credence. The Supreme Court further observed that the Judges who bear the sword of justice should not hesitate to use the sword of justice with utmost severity, to the full and to the end, if the gravity of the offence so demands. In *Dhananjoy Chatterji* v. *State of W.B.*[11] involving the commission of rape with murder of a young girl of age below 18 years, the Apex Court while confirming the death sentence awarded by the Courts below treated the case a "rare of the rarest" observed as under:

> "We agree that a real and abiding concern for the dignity of human life is required to be kept in mind by the Courts while considering the confirmation of the sentence of death but a cold-blooded pre-planned brutal murder without any provocation, after committing rape on an innocent and defenseless young girl of 18 years by the security guard certainly makes this case a rare of the rarest which calls for no punishment other than the capital punishment."

Where the accused committed rape on an infant child of 1¾ years in consequence of which she died and the trial Court awarded R.I. for life with fine under Section 376 sub-section (2) (f) IPC and death sentence under Section 302 I.P.C. with fine, the High Court in Murder reference no. 1 of 1993 and Criminal Appeal no. 162 DB of 1993 arising out the same Judgement,[12] declined to confirm the death sentence holding that this case does not appear to fall in the category of the rarest of rare cases so as to attract the extreme penalty of death, notwithstanding the gruesome nature of the offences involved. In the present case, the deceased died, due to shock and hemorrhage and pain due to rape on her, which was ante-mortem in nature and sufficient to cause death in the ordinary course of nature. The crime was committed for satisfying lust.

Where Nitma, a girl of tender age of 7 years who fell victim to a pray of his lust, by the accused who was none other than the paternal uncle of the deceased victim girl, the Supreme Court confirmed death sentence on the appellant and observed as under[13]

> "The Post-mortem over the dead body of the victim goes to show that she had several external and internal injuries on her person including a serious injury in her private parts showing the brutality with which she was subjected to while committing rape on her. The victim of the age of Nitma could not have ever resisted the act with which she was subjected to. The appellant seems to have acted in a beastly manner as after satisfying his lust he thought that the victim might expose him for the commission of the offence of forcible rape on her to the family members and others, the appellant with a view to screen the evidence of his crime and put an end to the life of the innocent girl who had seen only seven summers. The evidence on record is indicative of the fact as to how diabolically, the appellant had conceived of his plan and brutally executed it and such a calculation, cold-blooded and brutal murder of a girl of very tender age after committing rape on her would undoubtedly fall in the category of rarest of the rare cases attracting no punishment other than the capital punishment."

The respondent, a youngman aged 32 years was tried for committing rape on a minor girl aged 5 years and was sentenced to suffer imprisonment for five years, on the basis of the sole testimony of one eye-witness plus other circumstantial evidence. The High Court set aside the trial Court's judgement. In Appeal under Article 136 of the Constitution of India, by the State of U.P., before the Apex Court, the Supreme Court restored the Judgement of the trial Court and held that the acquittal of the respondent was totally unmerited and such unmerited acquittals, particularly in crimes against girl child encourage the criminals. The Courts, have, therefore, to be sensitive while dealing with such cases.[14]

7.07 Conclusion

In the metropolitan city of Delhi, during 1994, out of the total reported cases of 168 incidents of rape, 98 were committed against minors.[15] The savage treatment of a girl child, is a pointer to the degeneration of social and human values. Unfortunately the police is not only insensitive to such incidents but also a culprit in some cases. Among many cases to bring on the record is the rape of a Bangladeshi 12 year girl by six cops. Not only this, she was kept in Tihar Jail with hardened criminals and not provided any food for days. Her only fault was that she was a victim. The law permits cross-examination of a child victim for hours by strangers in unfamiliar surroundings.[15]

Mrs. Sarkar, a law professor has pointed out that in connection with the rape and murder case of an 11 year school girl, the police went to the school to verify the victims character. In Jhaku case, the police disbelieving the complaint about the rape of a daughter by father, held that a father cannot rape his own daughter and must be something wrong with the child.[15]

If not to prevent, but at least to minimise the incidence of child rape, there is a need for modification in procedural law for the trial and investigation of cases relating to child rape and also to provide stringent punishment besides policing the police.

The recommendations of the Committee of the National Federation for Indian Women (NFIW),[16] for amendment in the rape laws, especially children under the age-group below 12 years, suggests the prevention of trauma of children of the victims from further questioning by the insensitive police officers and men and lengthy processes during trial. These suggestions are within the frame-work of the existing law for minors. It has been suggested that the corroborative evidence like injury report, clothes of the victims and scientific evidence should receive a great weight if the child makes a statement to his or her parents or close relations.

There must be strict implementation of Sec. 309 Cr. P.C. dealing with the expeditious trial and examination of witnesses on day to day basis without long adjournments.

The recommendation also includes the deletion of the provision of Anticipatory Bail under Section 438 Cr.P.C. and the trial in case of rape by a Judge of the fair sex.

The Committee further recommended amendment of Sec. 439 and Sec. 401 of Cr.P.C. so that the victim's counsel enjoys the right to assist and address the Court alongwith the Public Prosecutor entrusted with the conduct of the prosecution case.

REFERENCES

1. Relevant Sections of I.P.C.

363A. Kidnapping or maiming a minor for purposes of begging: (1) Whoever kidnaps any minor or, not being the lawful guardian of a minor, obtains the custody of the minor, in order that such minor may be employed or used for the purposes of begging, shall be punishable with imprisonment of either description for a term which may extend to ten years, and shall also be liable to fine

(2) Whoever maims any minor in order that such minor may be employed or used for the purposes of begging shall be punishable with imprisonment for life, and shall also be liable to fine.

(3) Where any person, not being the lawful guardian of a minor, employs or uses such minor for the proposes of begging, it shall be presumed, unless the contrary is proved, that he kidnapped or otherwise obtained the custody of that minor in order that the minor might be employed or used for the purpose of begging.

(4) In this Section:

(a) begging means:
- (i) soliciting or receiving alms in public place, whether under the pretence of singing, dancing, fortune telling, performing tricks or selling articles or otherwise;
- (ii) entering on any private premises for the purpose of soliciting or receiving alms;
- (iii) exposing or exhibiting, with the object of obtaining or extorting alms, any sore, wound, injury, deformity or disease, whether of himself or of any other person or of an animal;
- (iv) using a minor as an exhibit for the purpose of soliciting or receiving alms;

(b) "minor" means
- (i) in the case of a male, a person under sixteen years of age; and
- (ii) in the case of a female, a person under eighteen years of age.

366. Kidnapping, abducting or inducing woman to compel her marriage, etc.: Whoever kidnaps or abducts any woman with intent that she may be compelled, or knowing it to be likely that she will be compelled, to marry any person against her will, or in order that she may be forced or seduced to illicit intercourse, or knowing it to be likely that she will be forced or seduced to illicit intercourse, shall be punished with imprisonment of either description for a term which extend to ten years, and shall also be liable to fine, and whoever, by means of criminal intimidation as defined in this Code or of abuse of authority or any other method of compulsion, induces any woman to go from any place with intent that she may be, or knowing that it is likely that she will be, forced or seduced to illicit intercourse with another person shall also be punishable as aforesaid.

366A. Procuration of minor girl: Whoever, by any means whatsoever, induces any minor girl under the age of eighteen years to go from any place or to any act with intent that such girl may be, or knowing that it is likely that she will be, forced or seduced to illicit intercourse with another person shall be punishable with imprisonment which may extend to ten years, and shall also be liable to fine.

366B. Importation of girl from foreign country: Whoever imports into India from any country outside India or from the State of Jammu and Kashmir any girl under the age of twenty-one years with intent that she may be, or knowing it to be likely that she will be forced or seduced to illicit intercourse with another person shall be punishable with imprisonment which may extend to ten years, and shall also be liable to fine.

372. Selling minor for purposes of prostitution, etc.: Whoever sells, lets to hire, or otherwise dispose of any person under the age of eighteen years with intent that such person at any age be employed or used for the purpose of prostitution or illicit intercourse with any person for any unlawful and immoral purpose, or knowing it to be likely that such person will at any age be employed or used for any such purpose, shall be punished with imprisonment of either description for a term which may extend to ten years, and shall also be liable to fine.

Explanation I: When a female under the age of eighteen years is sold, let for hire or otherwise disposed of to a prostitute or to any person who keeps or manages a brothel, the person so disposing of such female shall, until the contrary is proved, be presumed to have disposed of her with the intent that she shall be used for the purposes of prostitution.

Explanation II: for the purposes of this section "illicit intercourse" means sexual intercourse between persons not united by marriage or by any union or tie which, though not amounting to a marriage, is recognised by the personal law or custom of the community to which they belong or, where they belong to different communities, of both such communities, as constituting between them a quasi-marital relation.

373. Buying minor for purposes of prostitution, etc.: Whoever buys, hires or otherwise obtains possession of any person under the age of eighteen years with intent that such person shall at any age be employed or used for the purpose of prostitution or illicit intercourse with any person or for any unlawful and immoral purpose, or knowing it to be likely that such person will at any age be employed or used for any purpose, shall be punished with imprisonment of either description for a term which may extend to ten years, and shall also be liable to fine.

Explanation I: Any prostitute or any person keeping or managing a brothel who buys, hires or otherwise obtains possession of a female under the age of eighteen years shall, until the contrary is proved, be presumed to have obtained possession of such female with the intent that she shall be used for the purpose of prostitution.

Explanation II: "Illicit intercourse" has the same meaning as in Section 372.

375. Rape: A man is said to commit "rape" who except in the case hereinafter excepted, has sexual intercourse with a woman under circum-

stances falling under any of the six following descriptions:-
First: Against her will.
Secondly: Without her consent.
Thirdly: With her consent, when her consent has been obtained by putting her or any person in whom she is interested in fear of death or of hurt.
Fourthly: With her consent, when the man knows that he is not her husband, and that her consent is given because she believes that he is another man to whom she is or believes herself to be lawfully married.
Fifthly: With her consent, when, at the time of giving such consent, by reason of unsoundness of mind or intoxication or the administration by him personally or through another of any stupefying or unwholesome substance, she is unable to understand the nature and consequences of that to which she gives consent.
Sixthly: With or without her consent, when she is under sixteen years of age.

Explanation: Penetration is sufficient to constitute the sexual intercourse necessary to the offence of rape.

Exception: Sexual intercourse by a man, with his own wife, the wife not being under fiften years of age, is not rape.

376. Punishment for rape: (1) Whoever, except in the cases provided for by sub-section (2), commit rape shall be punished with imprisonment of either description for a term which shall not be less than seven years but which may be for life or for a term which may extend to ten years and shall also be liable to fine unless the woman raped is his own wife and is not under twelve years of age, in which case, he shall be punished with imprisonment of either description for a term which may extend to two years or with fine or with both:

Provided that the Court may, for adequate and special reasons to be mentioned in the judgment, impose sentence of imprisonment for a term of less than seven years.

(2) Whoever,

(a) being a police officer commits rape-

(i) within the limits of the police station to which he is appointed; or

(ii) in the premises of any station house whether or not situated in the police station to which he is appointed; or

(iii) on a woman in his custody or in the custody of a police or a police officer subordinate to him; or

(b) being a public servant, takes advantage of his official position and commits rape on a woman in his custody as such public servant or in the custody of a public servant subordinate to him; or

(c) being on the management or on the staff of a jail, remand home or other place of custody established by or under any law for the time being in force or of a woman's or children's institution takes advantage of his official position and commits rape on any inmate of such jail, remand home, place or institution; or

(d) being on the management or on the staff of a hospital takes advantage of his official position and commits rape on a woman in that hospital; or

(e) commits rape on a woman knowing her to be pregnant; or

(f) commits rape on a woman when she is under twelve years of age; or

(g) commits gang rape,

shall be punished with rigorous imprisonment for a term which shall not be less than ten years but which may be for life and shall also be liable to fine;

Provided that the court may, for adequate and special reasons to be mentioned in the judgment, impose a sentence of imprisonment of either description for a term of less than ten years.

Explanation 1: Where a woman is raped by one or more in a group of persons acting in furtherance of their common intention, each of the persons shall be deemed to have committed gang rape within the meaning of this sub-section.

Explanation 2: "Women's or Children's institution" means an institution, whether called an orphanage or a home for neglected women or children or a widow's home or by any other name, which is established and maintained for the reception and care of women or children.

Explanation 3: " Hospital" means the precincts of the hospital and includes the precincts of any institution for the reception and treatment of persons during convalescence or of persons requiring medical attention or rehabilitation.

377. Unnatural offence: Whoever has carnal intercourse against the order of nature with any man, woman or animal, shall be punished with imprisonment for life, or with imprisonment of either description for a term which may extend to ten years, and shall also be liable to fine.

Explanation: Penetration is sufficient to constitute the carnal intercourse necessary to the offence described in this Section.

2. Firoz Bakht Ahmad, *"No gender bias in the trade"*, *The Hindustan Times,* (Delhi Edn.) dated 12.8.95.
3. Ashis Nanda, *"Where Children become slaves, gussa Kyon Nahi Ayega?"*, *The Hindustan Times,* (Delhi Edn.), August 12, 1995.
4. Vigita Fernandes, *"Seashells and Sex on sale"*, *The Sunday Times of India Review* (Delhi Edn.) dt. 15.8.1993.
5. V.N. Kakar, "The Lost boys of Pakistan", *The Hindustan Times,* (Delhi Edn.) dated 19.11.95.
6. Mallika Akbar, "Abuse: A vicious circle", *The Sunday Times,* (Delhi Edn.), November 19, 1995.
7. *Rayassat v. State of U.P.,* II(1993) CCR 1369 (DB).
8. *Rayassat v. State of U.P.,* II(1993) CCR 1926 (DB).
9. Rajbir Singh A Raju v. State (Delhi Admn.) III (1993) CCR 2128.
10. JT 1992(3) SC 270: II(1992) CCR 88 (SC): 1992 (2) Crimes 168(SC).
11. I(1994) CCR 98(SC).
12. *State of Punjab* v. *Harchet Singh & Chet Singh,* I (1994) CCR 416(DB).
13. *Laxman Naik* v. *State of Orissa,* II (1994) CCR 299(SC).
14. *State of U.P.* v. *Babulnath,* III(1994) CCR 706 (SC).
15. H.T. Correspondent, "Compaign against Child Abuse", *The Hindustan Times,* (Delhi Edn.) dated 29.10.1995.
16. H.T. Correspondent, "Steps to strengthen laws on Child Rape", *The Hindustan Times,* (Delhi Edn.) dated 14.12.95.

Chapter VIII

JUSTICE FOR JUVENILE OFFENDERS

8.01 Introduction

The provision of Section 4 of the Code of Criminal Procedure[1] are applicable where the offence under the Indian Penal Code or under any other law is being investigated, inquired into, tried or otherwise dealt with.[2] But where a complete Code exists which prescribes procedure in the enactment for the trial etc. of such offence, it is that procedure which is applicable and should, therefore, be followed and not the one prescribed by the Code of Criminal Procedure, 1973; for instances offences under the Foreign Exchange Regulation Act, 1947. The provision of any special Act will override the procedure laid down in the usual Code of Criminal Procedure.[3] In the event of the absence of a particular offence, the same will have to be investigated, inquired into, tried and otherwise dealt with in accordance with the provisions of the Cr. P.C. The Cr. P.C., therefore has the status of the parent Statute in respect of investigation, inquiry and trial of cases by various Criminal Codes.[4]

8.02 Juvenile Defined

The expression Juvenile means to include such boys who have not attained the age of 16 years or such girls who have not attained the age of 18 years.[5] A child means a person under the age of 15 years.[6] The Children Act of 1960 defines child in the same way as the Section 2(h) of Juvenile Justice Act, 1986.[7] Therefore, a child and juvenile have the same legal definition.

8.03 Why Juveniles/Children are to be Given Special Treatment in the Trial of Criminal Offences?

A child is a national asset and, therefore, it is the duty of the State to look after the child with a view to ensuring full development of its personality. That is why all the statutes dealing with children provide that a child shall not be kept in jail. Even apart from this Statutory prescription, it is elementary that jail is hardly a place where a child should be kept. There can be no doubt that incarceration in jail would have the effect of dwarfing the development of the child, exposing him to the baneful influences concerning his conscious and alienating him from the society. It is a matter of regret that despite Statutory provisions and frequent exhortations by social scientists there are still large number of children in different jails in the country as is now evident from the reports of the survey made by the District Judges persuant to our orders dated the 15th August 1985. Even when the children are accused of an offence, they must not be kept in jails . . . . It is the atmosphere of the jail which has a highly injurious effect on the mind of the child, estranging him from the society and breeding in him aversion bordering on hatred against a system which keeps him in jail. We would, therefore, like once again to impress upon the State Governments that might set up necessary remand homes and observation homes where children accused of an offence can be lodged, pending investigation and trial.

The above observation has been made by Bhagwati, C.J.[8] after noticing the provisions of Article 39(f) of the Constitution of India.[9]

8.04 Jurisdiction for Trial of Juveniles

Section 27 of Cr.P.C.,1973,[10] provides for trial of juveniles by a Chief Judicial Magistrate or any Court specially empowered under the Children Act, 1960. The expressions, *"custody"*, *"trial"* and *"punishment"* occurring in Section 29(B) of 1898 Code has been replaced by *"treatment"*, *"training"* and *"rehabilitation"* in Section 27 of the 1973 Code.

In the State of Uttar Prasdesh, the U.P. Children Act, 1951 (U.P. Act no. 1 of 1951) received assent of the President on 5.2.1952. Section 60 of the U.P. Children Act, 1951, provides for establishment of Juvenile Court for any local area. Section 60(2)[11] describes what a Juvenile Court should be.

Various States have enacted their own children Acts providing procedures to deal with the trial of a child. Juvenile Courts constituted under the said Acts had the exclusive jurisdiction to try juveniles even for offences punishable with death or imprisonment for life. The Children Act, 1960 (Act 60 of 1960) was enacted for the welfare etc. of children, residing within the Union Territories of India, Section 5 of the said Act provides for Children's Court.[12] The Juvenile Justice Act, was enacted vide Act no. 53 of 1986—after coming into force of this Act, any law in any State corresponding to this law stood repealed. Section 5[13] of this Act provides for "Juvenile Court". Section 5 of both these Acts are identical in phraseology, except that the expressions *"children's"* and *'Administrator'* occurring in Children's Act have been replaced by *"Juvenile"* and *"State Government"* respectively in Juvenile Justices Act. The question is whether Section 27 of the Cr.P.C. takes away powers of the Children Court or the Juvenile Court? The M.P. High Court, in the context of M.P. Bal Adhiniyam Act has held that Section 26[14] of Cr.P.C., 1973 is void and a child must be tried for the offence punishable with death or transportation for life by a Court of Sessions in accordance with the new Cr.P.C.[15]

The Supreme Court, while considering a similar provision of Haryana Children Act over-ruled the Full Bench decision of the M.P. High Court and observed.[16]

> "Section 27 is not a specific provision within the meaning of Section 5[17] of the Code. The intention of the Parliament was not to exclude the trial of the delinquent children for offences punishable with death and imprisonment for life in as much as Section 27 does not contain expression to the effect notwithstanding anything contained in any Children Act passed by the State Legislature."
>
> "It was further observed that the relevant provisions of the Code and the Act can co-exist and their sphere of operation are different. By a combined reading of Section 5[17], 6[18] and 27[10] of Cr.P.C., 1973, it is evident that Section 27 of the Code does not, by implications, take away the power in respect of Juvenile Offender even for an offence punishable with death or imprisonment for life."

In the case of *Sheela Barse & Another* v. *U.O.I. & Others,*[19] the Supreme Court called upon the State Governments to bring into force and to implement vigorously the provisions of the Children Act enacted in the various States. It was observed:

> "But we would suggest that instead of each State having its own Children Act in different procedures and content from the Children's Act in other States, it would be desirable if the Central Government initiates Parliamentary Legislation on the subject, so that there is complete uniformity in regard to the various provisions relating to Children's Act which may be enacted by Parliament. The Act should contain not only provisions for investigation and trial of an offence against children below 16 years but should also contain mandatory provisions for ensuring social, economic and psychological rehabilitation of the children who are either accused of offences or abandoned, or destitutes or lost."

In accordance with the aforesaid direction of the Apex Court, Juvenile Justice Act, 1986 was enacted as a Central Act to deal with the problems of Juvenile delinquency in India. Thus the Juvenile Justice Act, 1986 (53 of 1986) came into force on 2.10.1987, in exercise of the powers conferred under sub-section (3) of Section 1 of the Juvenile Justice Act, 1986 by Notification No. GSR 710(E) dated the 13th August 1987. The Act extends to the whole of India except Jammu & Kashmir.[20]

8.05 Salient Features of Juvenile Justice Act, 1986

Section 5 of the Act provides for the constitution of Juvenile Courts by Notification by the State Government. Where no Board or Juvenile Court has been constituted, then in that situation, Section 7(2) makes provisions that the powers conferred on the Board or the Juvenile Court by or under this Act shall be exercised in that area only by the following:

(a) the District Magistrate; or
(b) the S.D.M.; or
(c) Any Metroplitan Magistrate or Judicial Magistrate of the First Class, as the case may be.

Section 7(3) of the Act provides that powers conferred on the Board or Juvenile Court by or under this Act may also be exercised by the High Court and the Court of Sessions when the proceeding comes up before them in appeal, revision or otherwise. The Juvenile Justice Act is a special enactment which deals with all cases of Juveniles. Section 63 of the Juvenile Justice Act repeals Children Act which was enforced in any State. The proviso to Section 63 which is important reads as under:

"(a) the previous operation of any law so repealed or anything duly done or suffered thereunder; or
(b) any right, privilege, obligation or liability acquired, accrued or incurred under any law as repealed; or
(c) any penalty, forfeiture or punishment incurred in respect of any offence committed against any law so repealed, or
(d) any investigation, legal proceeding or remedy in respect of any such right, privilege, obligation, liability, penalty, forfeiture or punishment as aforesaid;

and any such investigation, legal proceeding or remedy may be instituted, continued or enforced and any such penalty, forfeiture or punishment may be imposed, as if this Act had not been passed."

Enquiry about age

The most important question for the applicability of Juvenile Justice Act, 1986 is that the person should be within the age limit as prescribed under Section 2(h) of the Act at the time of the commission of the Act. The person may not be a juvenile at the time of the trial, still he will be tried and order passed in his case as if he had been a juvenile.[21] In determining the age, the Court should make proper enquiries including medical report and should not depend on the visual appearance of the accused.[22] Section 32(1) of the Act provides that where it appears to a Competent Authority that a person brought before it, is a juvenile and is accused of an offence, the Competent Authority shall take into consideration, the following circumstances,[23] namely:

(a) the age of the juvenile;
(b) the state of physical and mental health of the juvenile;
(c) the circumstances in which the juvenile was and is living;
(d) the reports made by the Probation Officers:
(e) the religious persuation of the juvenile:
(f) such other circumstances as may, in the opinion of the authority require to be taken into consideration in the interest of the welfare of the juvenile:

Provided . . ."

However, this does not mean that whenever any question about the age of an accused is raised in any Court other than the Juvenile Court during the course of trial or enquiry such Court must invariably refer the question to the Juvenile Court for determination of age.[24] Section 8(1) of the Juvenile Justice Act, provides that when any Magistrate, not empowered to exercise the powers of a Board or a Juvenile Court under the Act, is of opinion that a person brought before him under any of the provisions of the Act is a juvenile, he shall record such opinion and forward the juvenile and the record of the proceedings to the competent Authority having jurisdiction over the proceedings. In *Gopinath* v. *State of W.B.*,[25] the Supreme Court before whom the question of minority was raised at belated stage and referred the matter to the Sessions Judge for enquiry and after having got a finding of the subject being a juvenile, referred the matter to the Juvenile Court, the Supreme Court also entertained the plea that at that belated stage.

Bail and Custody of Juvenile

The provision of Section 18 of the Juvenile Justice Act,[26] entitles a person, who apparently appears to be a juvenile to be released on bail with or without surety when such person is brought before a Court. This provision over-rides the provision of the Code of Criminal Procedure and, therefore, is a special enactment.[27] A bare reading of the provision makes it abundantly clear ordinarily if a juvenile has to be released on bail irrespective of the nature of the offence alleged to have been committed by him unless it is shown that there appears reasonable ground for believing that his release is likely to bring him under the influence of any criminal or expose him to more dangers or that his release would defeat the ends of justice.[28] But a mere apprehension of creating terror or of tampering with the evidence is not sufficient to refuse bail.[29] Repetition of crime could be a ground for refusing bail[30] but where a juvenile delinquent was found to have committed a heinous offence of rape, bail was rejected.[31]

The N.D.P.S.* Act 1985, is a special enactment. Section 37(1) (b) of the said Act is about the limitations of bail which provides that no person accused of an offence punishable for an imprisonment

* Narcotic Drugs and Psychotropie Substances

of 5 years or more under the Act shall be released on bail or on his own bond subject to the twin conditions, viz: (i) an appourtunity to the Public Prosecutor to oppose the application of bail and (ii) the satisfaction of the Court that there are reasonable grounds for believing that he is not guilty of such offence and he is not likely to commit any offence while on the bail. Sub-section (2) provides that limitations of bail so specified in Clause (b) of Sub-section (1) are in addition to the limitation under the Code of Criminal Procedure. The provisions under the N.D.P.S. Act is rather a stringent measure but has been engrafted into the Statute book for the larger interest of the society. Thus, in order, to achieve the objective of curbing the menace and social evil and has been found to be dangerously affecting the back-bone of the country, release of an accused involved in the commission of an offence under the N.D.P.S. Act would defeat the ends of justice and the drug traffickers would pursue their objective of drug trafficking through the juvenile delinquents. While rejecting the bail of the petitioner, who was a juvenile, the High Court, with these words, recommended that the petitioner, who was a juvenile should not be kept in the same Cell as the hardened criminal but in a separate place to avoid mixing with hardened criminals.[32]

Action to be taken on the arrest of a juvenile

Action consequent upon the arrest of a juvenile required to be taken has been provided in Section 19 of the Juvenile Justice Act.[33] On production before a Juvenile Court, the court shall hold the enquiry in accordance with the provisions of Section 39[34] of the Act and may subject to the provisions of this Act, make such order in relation to the juvenile as it deems fit.[35]

Orders that may be passed in case of Delinquent Juvenile and prohibition against passing of certain Orders

Consequent upon the enquiry, a Juvenile Court may pass orders in accordance with the provisions of Section 21 of the Act.[36] Section 22 of the Act[37] mentions as to which orders may not be passed against the delinquent juvenile.

Prohibition of certain Proceedings against Juvenile Offenders

Section 23 of the Act prohibits the institution of proceedings and passing of an order against a juvenile under Chapter VIII of

Cr.P.C.[38] Section 24[39] prohibits joint trial of juvenile and a person not a juvenile. Section 25[40] bars the labelling of disqualification attached to the conviction.

8.06 Conclusion

On the conclusion of the trial, the Trial Court, if comes to the conclusion that accused, being a juvenile, has committed an offence, it shall after recording the finding forward the juvenile to the Juvenile Court as required by Section 26[41] of the Act. The Trial Court will have to give its finding about the age of the accused on the date when the offence is alleged to have been committed and for this purpose the Lower Court may, if necessary, refer the accused to the Medical Board or C.M.O. as the case may be for obtaining creditworthy evidence of age. The Lower Court may, as well, call upon the accused also to lead evidence about his age.[42]

The Juvenile Justice Act is much concerned about the welfare and rehabilitation of the juveniles. The Juvenile Justice Act even contains provisions regarding delinquent juvenile already undergoing sentence at the commencement of the Act. The benefit of the Juvenile Justice Act also gives to the juvenile whose trials have already been completed for sending the said delinquent to the special home or to be kept in safe custody by the State Government. This provision has been incorporated in Section 56 of the Act.[42]

It is thus clear from the scheme of the Act that any person found to be a child/juvenile shall not be sent to the jail and will not be treated at par with the adult accused persons or convicts.[42]

The Officer in Charge of the Police Stations, the Magistrates and the Courts should be extremely careful that any person accused of an offence, if apparently appeared to be a juvenile is arrested or appears or is brought before, them, the said persons should not be sent to jail and the provisions of this Act may be applied in letter and spirit.[42]

REFERENCES

1. "*Sec. 4 Cr.P.C.-Trial of offences under the Indian Penal Code and other Laws:* (1) All Offences under the Indian Penal Code (45 of 1860) shall be investigated, inquired into, tried, and otherwise dealt with according to the provisions hereinafter contained.

(2) All offences under any other law shall be investigated, inquired into, tried, and otherwise dealt with according to the same provisions, but subject to any enactment for the time being in force regulating the manner of place of investigating, inquiring into, trying or otherwise dealing with such offences."
(Corresponding law; Sec. 5 of Cr.P.C. 1898).

2. *Khatri* v. *State of Bihar*, AIR 1981 SC 1968.
3. *Nil Ratan sircar* v. *Lakshmi Narayan*, (1964) 7 SCR 724: 1965 (1) Cr L J 100: AIR 1965 SC 1.
4. *A.R. Antulay* v. *R.S. Nayak* AIR 1984 Sc 718.
5. Vide Sec. 2 (h) of the Juvenile Justice Act, 1986.
6. Vide Sec. 2(4) of U.P. Children Act, 1951, (Act. 1 of 1951).
7. Vide Sec. 2 (e) of Children Act, 1960.
8. *Sheela Barse & Another* v. *U.O.I. & Others*, AIT 1986 SC 1973.
9. Art. 39 (f) of the Constitution of India:

   39. Certain principles of policy to be followed by the State: The State in particular, direct its policy towards securing

   (f) that children are given opportunities and facilities to develop in a healthy manner and in conditions of freedom and dignity and that childhood and youth are protected against exploitation and against moral and material abandonment"-Subs. by Constitution Amendment Act, 1976, S. 7 w.e.f. 3.1.1977.
10. "*Sec. 27 of Cr.P.C.—jurisdiction in the case of Juveniles:*Any offence not punishable with death or imprisonment for life, committed by any person who at the date when he appears or is brought before the Court is under the age of sixteen years, may be tried by the Court of a Chief Judicial Magistrate, or by any Court specially empowered under the Children Act, 1960 (60 of 1960), or any other law for the time being in force providing for the treatment, training and rehabilitation of youthful offenders."
    (Corresponding Law; Sec. 29(B) of Cr.P.C. 1898.)
11. *Sec. 60(2) of U.P. Children Act, 1951. Juvenile Court:* (1) * * * * *

(2) For purposes of this Act, a Court means the Juvenile Court established by the State Government for any area and including a Court of Sessions and a Magistrate of the First Class specially empowered to exercise the powers of a Court under this Act.

12. Vice Sec. 5 of the Children Act, 1960.
13. Sec. 5 of the Juvenile Justice Act, 1986, reads as under:

    5. Juvenile Courts: (1) Notwithstanding anything contained in the code of Criminal Procedure, 1973, the State Government may, by notification in the Official Gazette, constitute for any area specified in the Notification, one or more Juvenile Courts for exercising the powers and discharging the duties conferred or imposed on such Court in relation to delinquent juveniles under this Act.

    (2) A Juvenile Court shall consist of such number of Metropolitan Magistrates or Judicial Magistrates of the First Class, as the case may be, forming a Bench as the State Government thinks fit to appoint, of whom one shall be designated as the Principal Magistrate; and every such Bench shall have the powers conferred by the Code of Criminal Procedure, 1973, on a Metropolitan Magistrate or, as the case may be, a Judicial Magistrate of the First Class.

(3) Every Juvenile Court shall be assisted by a panel of two honorary social workers possessing such qualifications as may be prescribed, of whom at least one shall be a woman, and such panel shall be appointed by the State Government.

14. Sec. 26 of Cr.P.C., 1973

26. Courts by which offences are triable—Subject to other provisions of this Code-

(a) any offence under the Indian Penal Code (45 of 1860) may be tried by-

(i) the High Court, or
(ii) the Court of Sessions, or
(iii) any other Court by which such offence is shown in the First Schedule to be triable;

(b) any offence under any other law shall, when any Court is mentioned, in this behalf in such law, be tried by such Court and when no Court is so mentioned, may be tried by

(i) the High Court, or
(ii) any other Court by which such offence in the First Schedule to be triable.

The U.P. State introduced the following amendment vide Act No. 1 of 1984 in Section 26(b)

For Clause (b) substitute the following:-

"(b) any offence under any other law may be tried:

(i) When any Court is mentioned in this behalf in such law, by such Court or by Court superior in rank to such Court, and
(ii) Where no Court is so mentioned, by any Court by which such offence is shown in First Schedule to be triable, or by any Court superios in rank to such Court."

15. *Debi Singh* v. *State of M.P.*, AIR 1978 MP 100 : 1978 Cr L J 585.
16. *Raghuvir* v. *State of Haryana,* AIR 1981 SC 2037: 181 SCC 809.
17. *Section 5 Cr.P.C.:* Saving—Nothing contained in this Code shall, in the absence of a specific provision to the contrary, affect any special or local law for the time being in force, any special jurisdiction or power conferred, or any special form of procedure prescribed, by any other law for the time being in force.
18. *Section 6 of Cr. P.C.:* Classes of Criminal Courts—Besides the High Courts and the Courts constituted under any law, other than this Code, there shall be, in every State, the following classes of Criminal Courts, namely:
    (i) Court of Sessions;
    (ii) Judicial Magistrates of the second class; and
    (iv) Executive Magistrates."
19. *Kamil* v. *State of U.P.*, II(1993) CCR 1100(1101)
20. AIR 1986 SC 1973.
21. Vide Section 3 of Juvenile Justice Act, 1986.
22. *Mubarak Ahmad* v. *State of U.P.*, III(1992) CCR 307.
23. Vide Section 33 of the Juvenile Justice Act, 1986.

24. *Sunil Dass & Another* v. *State of West Bengal,* III(1992) CCR 2524.
25. AIR 1984 SC 237.
26. Section 18 of the Act reads as under:-

18. Bail and Custody of Juveniles: (1) When any person accused of a bailable or non-bailable offence and apparently a juvenile is arrested or appears or is brought before a Juvenile Court, such person shall, notwithstanding anything contained in the Code of Criminal Procedure, 1973 (2 of 1974) or in any other law for the time being in force, be released with or without surety but he shall not be so released if there appear reasonable grounds for believing that his release is likely to bring him into assocuation with any known criminal or expose him to moral danger or that his release would defeat the ends of justice.

(2) When such person having been arrested is not released on bail by the officer-in-charge of the police station, such officer shall cause him to be kept in an observation home or a place of safety in the prescribed manner (but not in a police station or jail) until he can be brought before a Juvenile Court.

3. When such person is not released on bail under sub-section (1) by the Juvenile Court, it shall, instead of committing him to prison, make an order sending him to an observation home or a place of safety for such period during the pendency of the inquiry regarding him as may be specified in the order.

27. *Antaryami Patra* v. *State of Orissa,* III(1993) CCR 2176.
28. *Navin Panwar* v. *The State* (Del. Admn.) II (1994) CCR 1026.
29. *Daya* v. *State of M.P.,* 1993(2) Crimes 201.
30. *Guddu* v. *The State of U.P.,* 1990 Cr L J 1531.
31. *Kalyan* v. *State of Rajasthan* 1981 Cr L J 1472.
32. *Antaryami Patra* v. *State of Orissa,* III (1993) CCR 2176.
33. Section 19 of the Act reads as under:

19. Information to parents or guardian or probation Officer—Where a juvenile is arrested, the officer-in-Charge of the police station to which the juvenile is brought shall, as soon as may be after the arrest, inform

(a) the parent or guardian of the juvenile, if he can be found, of such arrest and direct him to be present at the juvenile Court before which the juvenile will appear: and

(b) the probation officer of such arrest in order to enable him to obtain information regarding the antecedents and family history of the Juvenile and other material circumstances likely to be of assistance to the Juvenile Court for making the inquiry.

34. Section 39 of the Act reads as under:-

39. Procedure in inquiries appeals and revision proceedings: (1) Save as otherwise expressly provided in this Act, a Competent authority while holding any inquiry under any of the provisions of this Act, shall follow, as far as may be, the procedure laid down in the Code of Criminal Procedure, 1973 (2 of 1974) for trial in summons cases.

(2) Save as otherwise expressly provide by or under this Act, the procedure to be followed in hearing appeals or revision proceedings under this Act shall be, as far as practicable, in accordance with the provisions of the Code of Criminal Procedure, 1973 (2 of 1974).

35. Section 20 of the Act reads as under:

20. Inquiry by Juvenile Court regarding delinquent juvenile: Where a juvenile having been charged with an offence appears or is produced before a juvenile Court, the Juvenile Court shall hold the inquiry in accordance with the provisions of Section 39 and may, subject to the provisions of this Act, make such order in relation to the juvenile as it deems fit.

36. Section 21 of the Act reads as under:

21. *Orders that may be passed regarding delinquent juveniles*

(1) Where a Juvenile Court is satisfied on inquiry that a juvenile has committed an offence, then, notwithstanding to the contrary contained in any other law for the time being in force, the Juvenile Court may, if it so thinks fit,

(a) allow the juvenile go to home after advice or admonition;

(b) direct the juvenile to be released on probation of good conduct and placed under the care of any parent, guardian or other fit person, on such parent, guardian or other fit person executing a bond, with or without surety as that Court may require, for the good behaviour and well-being of the juvenile for any period not exceeding three years;

(c) direct the juvenile to be released on probation of good conduct and placed under the care of any fit institution for the good behaviour and well-being of the juvenile for any period not exceeding three years;

(d) make an order directing the juvenile to be sent to a special home,-

(i) in the case of a boy over fourteen years of age or of a girl over sixteen years of age, for a period of not less than three years;

(ii) in the case of any other juvenile, for the period until he ceases to be a juvenile:

Provided that the Juvenile Court may, if it is satisfied that having regard to the nature of the offence and the circumstances of the case it is expedient so to do, for reasons to be recorded, reduce the period of stay to such period as it thinks fit:

Provided further that the Juvenile Court may, for reasons to be recorded, extend the period of such stay, but in no case the period of stay shall extend beyond the time when the juvenile attains the age of eighteen years, in the case of a boy, or twenty years, in the case of a girl;

(e) order the juvenile to pay a fine if he is over fourteen years of age and earns money.

(2) Where an order under clause (b), clause (c) or clause (e) of sub-section (1) is made, the Juvenile Court may, if it is of opinion that in the interests of the juvenile and of the public it is expedient so to do, in addition make an order that the delinquent juvenile shall remain under the supervision of a probation officer named in the order during such period, not exceeding three years, as may be specified therein, and may in such supervision order impose such conditions as it deems necessary for the due supervision of the delinquent juvenile:

Provided that if at any time afterwards it appears to the Juvenile Court on receiving a report from the probation officer or otherwise, that the delinquent juvenile has not been of good behaviour during the period of supervision or that the fit institution under whose care the juvenile was placed is no longer able or willing to ensure the good behaviour and well-being of the juvenile it may, after making such inquiry as it deems fit, order the delinquent juvenile to be sent to a special home.

(3) The Juvenile Court making a supervision order under sub-section (2), shall explain to the juvenile and the parent, guardian or other fit person or fit institution, as the case may be, under whose care the juvenile has been placed, the terms and conditions of the order and shall forthwith furnish one copy of the supervision order to the juvenile, the parent, guardian or other fit person or fit institution as the case may be, the sureties, if any, and the probation office.

(4) In determining the special home, or any person or institution to whose custody a juvenile is to be committed or entrusted under this Act, the Court shall pay due regard to the religious denomination of the juvenile to ensure that religious instruction contrary to the religious persuasion of the juvenile is not imparted to him.

37. Section 22 of the Act reads as under:

22. *Orders that may not be passed against delinquent juveniles*

(1) Notwithstanding anything to the contrary contained in any other law for the time being in force, no delinquent juvenile shall be sentenced to death or imprisonment, or committed to prison in default of payment of fine or in default of furnishing security:

Provided that where a juvenile who has attained the age of fourteen years has committed an offence and the Juvenile Court is satisfied that the offence committed is of so serious a nature or that his conduct and behaviour have been such that it would not be in his interest or in the interest of other juvenile in a special home to send him to such special home and that none of the other measures provided under this Act is suitable or sufficient, the Juvenile Court, may order the delinquent juvenile to be kept in safe custody in such place and manner as it thinks fit and shall report the case for the orders of the State Government.

(2) On receipt of a report from a Juvenile Court under sub-section (1), the State Government may make such arrangement in respect of the juvenile as it deems proper and may order such delinquent juvenile to be detained at such place and on which conditions at is thinks fit:

Provided that the period of detention so ordered shall not exceed the maximum period of imprisonment to which the juvenile could have been sentenced for the offence committed.

38. Chapter VIII of Cr.P.C., 1973 (2 of 1974) relates to the "Security for keeping peace and for the good behaviour" and embraces in its fold nineteen sections (Sections 106–124).

39. Section 24 of the Act reads as under:

24. No joint trial of juvenile and person not a juvenile- (1) Notwithstanding anything contained in Section 223 of the Code of Criminal Procedure, 1973 (2 of 1974), or in any other law for the time being in force, no juvenile shall be charged with or tried for any offence together with a person who is not a juvenile.

(2) If a juvenile is accused of an offence for which under Section 223 of the Code of Criminal Procedure, 1973, or any other law for the time being in force, such juvenile and any person who is not a juvenile would, but for the prohibition contained in sub-section (1), have been charged and

tried together, the Court taking cognizance of that offence shall direct separate trials of the juvenile and the other person.

40. Section 25 of the Act reads as under:

25. Removal of disqualification attaching to conviction- Notwithstanding anything contained in any other law, a juvenile who has committed an offence and has been dealt with under the provisions of this Act shall not suffer disqualifications, if any, attaching to a conviction of an offence under such law.

41. Section 26 of the Act reads as under:

26. Special provision in respect of pending cases: Notwithstanding anything contained in this Act, all proceedings in respect of a juvenile pending in any Court in any area on the date on which this Act comes into force in that area, shall be continued in that Court as if this Act has not been passed and if the Court finds that the juvenile has committed an offence, it shall record such finding and instead of passing any sentence in respect of the juvenile forward the juvenile to the Juvenile Court which shall pass orders in respect of that juvenile in accordance with the provisions of this Act as if it had been satisfied on inquiry under this Act that the juvenile has committed that offence.

42. Kamil v. The State of U.P., II(1992) CCR 1100(1107-80)

CHAPTER IX

HEALTH CARE AND NUTRITION

9.01 Introduction

Article 47 of the Constitution of India, guarantees the raising of the level of nutrition and the improvement of the public health as among its primary duties.

Article 24(2) *"On the Convention on the Rights of Child"* which was adopted by the General Assembly of the United Nations on 20.11.1989, the State parties including the Government of India have acceded to persue the full implementation to:[1]

(a) diminish infant and child mortality;
(b) to ensure the provision of necessary medical assistance and health care to all children and primary health care; and
(c) to combat disease and malnutrition including primary health care and through adequate nutritious food and clean drinking water.

9.02 Factors Affecting Health and Nutrition Problems in Developing Countries [2]

Besides lack of food, the biggest contributing factor which is a threat to nutritional health is illness. Illness depresses the appetite and reduces the system's capability to absorb and digest the food eaten. Another major factor is the overall quality of child care and child feeding practices. As a matter of fact, breast feeding is the most appropriate food for the child and no other food is a match to it. Malnutrition can be defeated through the availability of adequate food, the prevention and control of disease and the well-informed care and feeding of young children.

9.03 Effect of Malnutrition

A programme was undertaken by the Regional Director of Nutrition of South Asia on nutritional issues in 1994.[3] As a sequel to that investigation the following facts have come to light.

(1) One-third of the developing world's children suffer from protein-energy malnutrition.
(2) An estimated 2,50,000 children lose their eyeshight per year on account of the lack of vitamin A.
(3) Lack of iodine in food results in the impaired development of 50 million children and causes an estimated one lakh infants to be born as cretin. A total of 1.6 billion people are at risk with consequences ranging from goitre to reduced mental and physical performance.
(4) Millions of infants are exposed to illness, poor growth and early deaths on account of the decline in breast-feeding.

9.04 Malnutrition Deaths[3]

Recent research has borough to surface that out of 1,30,00,000 children under five years of age dying every year in the world, an estimated 55 per cent deaths do take place due to malnutrition.

In the developing countries, measles, diarrhoea and pneumonia are the greatest enemies to the children's health. On account of the poor nutrition, approximately 7 million children are killed every year and leave millions more mal-nutritioned. Diseseases like polio, measles, pneumonia and tetanus take a large toll of children.

Polio: The virus at its height crippled some 6,50,000 children in a year but after the discovery of vaccine in mid-sixties, this figure has come down to 1,50,000. The 80 per cent target for polio immunization have been reached by 80 countries and a total of 5 countries have already reached the 90 per cent coverage target set for the year 2000 A.D.

Measles: During the middle of the century, some tens of millions of children were affected every year killing approximately seven million children and leaving many of the survivors prey to malnutrition, diarrhoea, and pneumonia. The figure in respect of death toll has now been brought down to one million due to the enforcement of levels of measles immunization. The efforts have remained steady on account of constant vigil on it and has met the 80 per cent target by 1990.

Tetanus: Tetanus accounts for the death of six lakhs babies in their infancy and takes a toll of fifty thousand mothers per year.

Tetanus deaths are caused by lack of proper hygeine during child birth, allowing tetanus spore to come into contact with the umbilical chord. Improved hygeine and immunization of pregnant women against tetanus can protect both mother and the new-born child.

Pneumonia: The annual death toll on account of pneumonia is over 3 million child per year. Out of the 3.6 million pneumonia deaths 80 per cent take place in 18 developing countries falling in the Zone of Africa and Asia. The figures for under-five children deaths on account of this disease in five countries of the Indian sub-continent during the year 1990 is as under:

Table 9.1

Countries	Total number of deaths	No. of under 5 deaths per 1000 of population
India	10,26,000	9
Pakistan	2,77,000	13
Bangladesh	2,81,000	16
Afghanistan	86,000	29
Nepal	43,000	13

AIDS: Acquired Immune Deficiency Syndrome (AIDS) is a disease which has been discovered recently and a detailed survey so far as the spread of disease among the children of Asian countries do not seem to have been made.

In 1994, the United States Bureau of the Census published estimates of the impact of the epidemic on long term population growth in the 13 African countries and three other countries,

Thailand, Brazil and Haiti and published an estimate of under-five deaths in the year 2010 and according to this report, in the year 2010, the number of under-five deaths on account of AIDS is likely to go up to 20,82,000 as against 12,34,000 due to other causes. The number of deaths with AIDS only, therefore, is estimated to be larger by 8,48,000 heads.[4]

In order to contain the spread of AIDS effectively efforts are desired to be taken without any delay.

Anaemic deaths: Anaemia results from iron deficiency. Anaemia is a major cause of death in pregnancy and childbirth. It affects more than 40 per cent of the developing world's women. If only pregnant women are taken into consideration, the ratio goes beyond 55 per cent. The worst affected area is South Asia, where an estimated 60 per cent of all women suffer from anaemia. During pregnancy, the requirement of iron in diet rises steeply. It is estimated that in that situation 75 per cent of all women become anaemic.[5]

Pregnancy anaemia rates in India has gone up to 83 per cent. It is nearly five times of the anaemia rate in United States which is 17 per cent.

9.05 Conclusion

The accompanying Table (9.02) gives relevant data in respect of seven Asian Countries for the year 1992 as regards population, population of under sixteen children, number of children born per thousand of the population, no. of under five deaths and the percentage of children under-weight.

It will be seen that in Asian Countries, the percentage of children is approximately 42 per cent of total population with highest in Pakistan at 46 per cent and the figures for Sri Lanka is the lowest which is 34 per cent. The figure for India is 38 per cent. The end of Century-goal agreed to by almost all the countries of the world following the 1990 World Summit for Children are in the zone of ten top-priority areas: These are:[6]

"1. A one-third reduction in under-five death rates.
2. A 50 per cent reduction in maternal mortality rates.
3. A halving of severe and moderate malnutrition among the world's under-fives, the elimination of micro-nutrient

Table 9.02: Stastistical Profile (1992) in Relation to South-Asian Countries[7]

Country	Total population in thousands	Children (under 16) population in thousands	Children population per thousand of the population	Annual no. of births in thousands	Annual no. of births per thousand of the population	Annual no. of under 5 deaths, in thousands	No. of under 5 deaths per 1000 of the population	Percentage of children under-weight
Afghanistan	19100	8200	429	1031	54	265	14	—
Bangladesh	119300	51500	432	4623	39	587	49	66
Bhutan	1600	700	437	65	40	13	8.1	38
India	879000	330800	377	25900	29	3213	3.7	63
Nepal	20600	9400	456	778	38	100	5.3	—
Pakistan	124800	57300	459	5117	41	701	5.6	40
Sri Lanka	17700	6000	339	371	21	7	4.0	29

Average: 418 Children per thousand for South Asian Countries.

disorders, support for breast-feeding by all hospitals and maternity units, and a reduction in the incidence of low birth weight to less than 10 per cent.

4. Achievement and maintenance of at least 90 per cent immunization coverage for infants, and universal tetanus immunization for women in the child-bearing years; the eradication of polio, the elimination of neonatal tetanus, a 90 per cent reduction in measles cases, and a 95 per cent reduction in measles deaths (compared to levels before immunization).
5. Achievement of 80 per cent Oral Rehydration Therapy (ORT) use and a halving of child deaths caused by diarrhoea.
6. A one-third reduction in child deaths from acute respiratory infections.
7. Basic education for all children and completion of primary education by at least 80 per cent—girls as well as boys.
8. Safe water and sanitation for all families.
9. Acceptance and observance, in all countries of the Convention on the Rights of the Child.
10. Family planning and services to be made available to all."

In the event if the target set aforesaid is achieved, by the end of this Century, much work has been done in the interest of the children.

REFERENCES

1. Article 24. Convention on the Rights of Child, (See Appendix 1).
2. Resource Material, "Literature on the Progress of Nation, 1994"—UNICEF.
3. Urban Jonason, "Millions Lost to Wrong Strategies", Literature on the Progress of Nation, p. 6–7.
4. Peter Adamson, "One Small step for a Summit"—The Progress of the Nation—UNICEF, p. 3 (5).
5. Urban Jonsson, "Millions Lost to Wrong Strategies—Over half pregnant women are anaemic" The Progress of Nations, (1994), p. 11.
6. Source Material, "National Performance Gaps—Statistical Profiles—South-East Asia"—The Progress of Nations p. 52.
7. *Ibid*. p. 53.

Chapter X

OTHER FORMS OF CRIME

10.01 Kidnapping

Kidnapping means stealing of a human being. 'Kid' means child. Section 361 of the I.P.C. [1] defines kidnapping as taking away or enticing a male under sixteen years of age or a female under eighteen years of age or any person of unsound mind from the lawful guardianship without the guardian's consent.

Some fifty years ago, in the Eastern part of the country, there used to be a talk about a class of persons known as *"Lakarsunghwa"*. Such person would be moving about with a piece of wood shaped as stick and besmeared with a quantity of intoxicant and a big cloth bag. Whenever such person would find a lonely child moving about, he would make the child smell the piece of wood, in consequence the child would become unconscious and thereafter it would be lifted, packed in the cloth bag and carried away. Such children, as per rumors current in those days, were either sacrificed at the root of the foundation of a large bridge under construction or recruited in the rank of hermits. One can find mention of such child-lifter in Tagore's short story *'Kabuliwallah'*. The story has been written in first person, and revolves round a *Kabuliwallah* who sells dry fruits in the streets of the city and is carrying a large cloth bag. The author's daughter Mini, a small girl, is afraid to go near the *'Kabuliwallah'* as she thinks him to be a child-lifter and the *'Kabulliwallah'* sees in Mini the image of his own daughter whom he had left at his native place where he is not able to go as he is unable to collect the amount required for the journey to Kabul from Bengal. In course of time, Mini is out of the hesitation and both, *'Kabuliwallah'* and Mini continue to chat for hours together almost every day.

In this connection, the authors can say that they neither came across any such *Lakarsunghwa* or know any specific case of such child-lifting .

Since eighties, the incidents of kidnapping of children have become rampant. The same is taking place either for ransom or to wreck vengeance or to dictate terms to the parents or guardian for some undue favour. Kidnapping for ransom is always with a threat if the stipulations were not met or money not paid or if the parents or guardian approached the police, the child would be killed. Perhaps the cue for such indulgence is derived from films screened now-a days.

Kidnapping is inhuman and such acts have no religious sanctions anywhere. Whatever the cause—cultural, social, religious or political, kidnapping deserved to be decried as the most despicable act. A person is taken off-guard or by deceit and then using that person's life and safety as a bargaining point is a condemnable act. Pressure is exerted on another party to yield to some demands. This is a blatantly treacherous act which can never be approved as a means to achieve a noble or rightful purpose.

The Greek philosopher and biographer, Plutarch (46–120 AD),[2] has mentioned an incident in one of his books, which throws light on this matter. Roman army had once laid siege to a fort. After a while, a man emerged from the fort bringing along some children. He approached the Roman Commander and introduced himself as tutor of the children from the royal family which was under siege inside the fort.

The Commander declared, "We shall achieve our aims through our valour. We shall not resort to cowardice and treachery." Such were the noble principles of the Romans which helped them to maintain their great empire from 890 BC to 500 AD, that is; for 1300 years.

On account of the rampant incidents of kindnappings for ransom, in the Criminal Law (Amendment) Act of 1993, Section 364-A has been inserted which provides punishment of imprisonment for life or death, with fine in cases of kidnapping for ransom etc.[3] However, it has no impact on criminals.

10.02 Child Murders

It has been seen that when a person is mentally or emotionally disturbed or if he is under a superstitious belief he does not hesitate to kill a hapless child. The following incidents are quoted here by way of examples:[4]

1. "One year old Kunhikannan, the youngest child and the only son out of the four children in the family was killed by his father Velayudhan, a popular school teacher of a Government School in a district of Palghat (Kerala) on 19.8.1987. After killing, the father sat, kept the severed head of the child in his lap, closed his eyes and it appeared that he went in deep meditation. This happened because something had been worrying Velayudhan and he had become a mental patient. The state of his mind did not change even after his marriage and he began to believe that some evil spirits were hovering around it. He started consulting sorcerers and became a victim of witch-craft. He was made to believe that the only way to get out of the trauma was by sacrificing his son Kunhikannan. It may not be out of place to mention that the child was the family's favourite as the word Kunhikannan means cynosure."

2. In another case, Vijayalakshmi, the mother of two sons aged 13 and 6 years and two daughters aged 9 and four years, on account of extreme poverty the threw her children in a well and, thereafter, herself jumped into well to commit suicide. She and her son were rescued from meeting the watery grave but the two daughters could not be saved. She was awarded punishment by the trial Court and the High Court in appeal sympathetically let her off with the punishment already undergone to meet the ends of justice and remarked as under about the pathetic condition:[5]

> "This is an unfortunate case where a crime on account of poverty, has led to two young lives meeting their ends in an unfortunate manner, having been thrown inside a well by the very mother who brought them into the world. Sometimes poverty and starvation lead to parents, not wanting their children to suffer, attempting to put an end to their lives knowing fully well that it is contrary to law. The parents suffer from a phobia that by killing them they would achieve the objective of putting an end to their sufferings, little realising that the parents' lifelong sufferings would start thereafter."

3. The gruesome murder of child is confined not only to India, where the same takes place on account of superstitions and poverty, but it extends to other countries as well. According to a report,[6] children are murdered every day in Brazil. While the general murder rate has decreased in Rio-de-Janeiro since 1990, more children are being murdered. 306 children died in 1991, 424 in the next year and in the first six months of 1993, the number leaped to 298.

The grim statistics usually get tucked away in the crime pages of the tabloids. During the first week of August 1993 eight street children were shot dead in the centre of Rio-de-Janeiro during midnight. The children were aged between 11 and 17, were all poor, most of them were black.

Observers guess that from 2,00,000 to 3 million children spend their days and often their nights on the streets. Many have houses but not homes, relations but no real family. Many of the killings are due to wars between drug gangs as well as the police, often at the behest of merchants, tired of hold-ups and breakings, often carried out by the minors.

4. Amar Singh, a Wazirpur slum dweller, apparently murdered his one year daughter, Amrita in an inebriated state presumably on account of the quarrel with his wife Gita due to his drinking habits. The wife shifted to her mother's nearby jhuggi. Within a couple of days of her shifting to the new place, the accused went there one afternoon, forcibly took his daughter from the mother and immersed her head in water which caused the death of the child, due to drowning. The police registered a case against Amar Singh.[7]

10.03 Child's Marriage

Not only the child marriage is banned in India but the marriage age has been raised to 21 years for the boys and 18 years for the girls. Child marriage is bad for the health of the children as well as the adolescents. In addition, the country cannot afford the luxury of child marriage on account of its over-grown population. Inspite of it, the child marriages are openly being performed on regular basis in the the State of Rajasthan. Unfortunately the State does not take any cognizance of the fact. A study undertaken by Family Planning Foundation of India (FPFI) during the closing years of the eighties have estimated that there were more than one crore girls who were married when they were not even 11 years of age.

For a girl, marriage is the most important problem and on account of the difficulties of the parents/guardian in locating suitable bridegrooms for their aged and educated girls and the inability to pay prices of such grooms, the girl's parents clear off this obligation through early marriage. According to a report almost all the daughters of Dumma village in Deograh (Bihar) district become brides before they attain the age of ten years. The elders of village hold that poverty is responsible for the rampant child marriage. The cost of marriage is directly proportional to the age of the girl. The chain effects lead to early motherhood and quick growth of population. The absence of any health support system for pregnant women and frequent spells of pregnancy often lead to fatality to the already malnourished and anaemic mothers, infant mortality and pregnancy deaths.[8]

10.04 Humiliating Situations

The children, at times have to face humiliating situations in schools and elsewhere. The following are cited by way of example:

1. The headmaster of the Government Higher Secondary School at Kuchchanoor near Uthamapalayam in Madurai district indiscriminately cut the locks of hairs of twenty-five school students including many girls students. The Headmaster had chased the children with a pair of scissors on that day and cut their hairs. The result was that many of boys had tonsure their heads while the girls remained confined to their homes as they were ashamed to come out of their houses.[9]

2. The Muslim majority schools in the State of Kerala are entitled to have Fridays as their weekly holidays instead of the usual Sundays. The C.T.S. School in Chavakad, a Taluk of Trissoor district, which is better known as mini Gulf because of the large number of its emigrants sending hefty petro-dollar remittances, fell just two short of the number of Muslim students prescribed for being qualified as a Muslim school. Two students, Savitha and Pradeep had to change their names to Sabeena and Wahab respectively under advise to enable the school not only to have Friday as the weekly holiday instead of Sunday but also to receive sizeable amounts of grants from various Islamic educational and other organizations, which in turn, receive liberal do-

nations from Keralites settled in the West-Asaian countries. This coercion by the school authorities came to light as a police case was registered in this context.

10.05 The Trauma of Adoption

When a person is not blessed with a child, the void created in life of the couple can be filled through adoption. The relevant legal provision for this purpose is "The Hindu Adoption and Maintenance Act, 1956" which is applicable to all Hindus and to any person who is not a Muslim, Christian, Parsi or Jew. The requisites for a valid adoption, in accordance with Section 6 of the Act are:

(i) the person adopting has the capacity and also the right, to take in adoption;
(ii) the person giving in adoption has the capacity to do so;
(iii) the person adopted is capable of being taken in adoption; and
(iv) the adoption is made in compliance with the other conditions mentioned in this Chapter.

The other requisites and conditions of a valid adoption are provided by Sections 10[10] and 11[11] of the Act. However, adoption may be traumatic for the adopted child in certain situations mentioned below.[12]

1. Saugandh was happy in his comforting family concoon as the only son of his doting parents. When he attained the age of eighteen years, his adoptive parents thought that the boy was mature enough and divulged that he was their adopted child but could not tell anything about his parentage except that he was adopted from an orphanage. The mental trauma of the child began after that on account of the feeling that he was probably an illegitimate child who was abandoned by his parents. Therefore, he was a bastard and what will happen, if his friends would come to know of this.

The second thought was that even if he was not a bastard child, he certainly was a child who was not loved by his real parents. The feeling of being totally rejected by the natural parents is associated with the feeling of inadequacy and lack of confidence in facing people.

The fact that the adoptive parents had never chastised the child in the life of Saugandh gave rise to the feeling that on account of his being an adopted child he was not chastised for anything. There is, however, the other side of the story as well. If the child is chastised, for his omissions and commissions, intended to correct him, he may gather the feeling that on account of not being a real child of the parents, he was being scolded.

Whether a child should be told about his being adopted is an important question. According to some, it should never be told, if the child does not know it. However, according to some people he should be told the moment he starts understanding. This is because, if the child learns of it, from some persons like the relations of his adoptive parents, it may perhaps be shocking to him to know of it.

Therefore, the method and style of communicating the story of adoption is important and should be decided according to circumstances commensurate with the personality and temperament of the child. What is important is that the child should not get the feeling of being rejected by anybody otherwise there could be many psychological and behavioural problems resulting in menifestation of bad habits in some cases.

2. However, the real trouble may start in later part of the life. When a childless couple adopts a child and later on they are blessed with a child of their own. "There is every chance of the adopted child being neglected."

Adoption is advantageous for an orphan who is benefited by becoming a member of a family and gets better monetary support. What is more important is that the emotional security of love, care, unity, togetherness and harmony should be of the same fibre that welds and comments a natural family. The expected care should not be belied by the subsequent distress and anguish that a child can feel after knowing about his adoption.

10.06 Minor's Guardianship and Custody

A minor is one who has not completed the age of 18 years[13] and since a minor is supposed to be of immature mind, the person and the property of the minor has to be put under the care of a guardian. The natural guardian of a Hindu minor, in accordance with Section 6 of the Hindu Minority and Guardianship Act,

1956, in respect of a boy or an unmarried girl is father and after him, the mother, provided that the custody of a minor below the age of five years rests ordinarily with the mother. The custody of an illegitimate boy or an illegitimate unmarried girl rests with the mother and after her, with father. In case of a married girl, the husband becomes the guardian. For this purposes, the step-mother and step-father are excluded from the status of mother and father respectively.

The adoptive father and after him, the adoptive mother are the natural guardian of an adopted son.[14]

In appointing a guardian by the Court, the welfare of the child/minor is of paramount importance.[15]

Even in the face of such strict provisions of law, at times, awkward situations are faced by children/minors. The recent news report of a tiny girl born in Shimla Sanitorium and Hospital during mid-1995 and her abandonment by the mother after four days of the birth is a classical example of this. She is being looked after by half a dozen 'foster' mothers, who are none other than the hospital nurses. The baby is kept on milk and cerelac food and has now started recognising her foster mothers.

The child at this age is fighting for her human rights. The State Human Rights Commission was seized of the matter through an undisclosed source and the matter is being probed by the Chairman of the State Human Rights Commission. Proper security for the child through cordoning off the area has been made to guard against the child being taken away illegally. The fate of the child will be decided after the completion of the probe by the Human Rights Commission.[16]

There is yet another complex case reported from Ajmer (Rajasthan) where a six year old girl, a student of Upper K.G. is locked in a custody case between her mother Smt. Usha Devi, a widow, another woman Mrs. Gita Devi, who claims herself to be the grand-mother of the child and Kumawats, the next door neighbour of the child's father Mr. Brahmdeo Sharma.

Mrs. Usha Devi was married to Mr. Brahmdeo Sharma, a social worker, and out of this wedlock, the couple had a son and the daughter in question. When the couple could not pull on well, then soon after the birth of this girl, Mrs. Usha Devi deserted her husband and before leaving him, she made over the daughter to Kumawat family, a next door neighbour after completing the formality of handing over of the daughter on a five-rupee stamp paper and she herself took away the son with her. The Kumawat family later on shifted to its own house built in another locality and got the girl admitted to a school with other two children of the family. Things were going on well peacefully.

Suddenly the Kumawats received a notice from the Court asking them to be present with the child as two claimants, Mrs. Usha Devi, the child's mother and one Mrs. Gita Devi claiming to be the grand-mother of the child sought the custody of the child. Mrs. Gita Devi alleged that the Kumawats have kidnapped the child and was keeping with them. The child, not knowing as to what was happening, had to attend the Court for the whole of December 1995 instead of her school. The matter was finally disposed off by Smt. Urmila Varma, the Judicial Magistrate, who first talked to the child in her chamber. The child refused to recognise Mrs. Usha Devi as her mother and recognised Kumawats as her parents. The Judicial Magistrate held that she had no authority to decide the issue. The parties were directed to approach the competent court.

Though for the time being, there is no Court case but the Kumawats are apprehensive of the fact that the two claimants may approach competent court for the custody of the child who otherwise is living peacefully under proper care of Kumawats.[17]

10.07 Special Homes for Juveniles

Where a Juvenile Court is satisfied that a juvenile has committed an offence, the Court may, under the provision of Section 21(1) (d) of Juvenile Justice Act make an order directing the juvenile to be sent to a special home. The provision has been made with a purpose to prevent the intermixing of juvenile offenders with hardened criminals. It is obligatory for the State to provide suitable special homes for the juveniles consistent with the rules. Rule 20 of J.J. Rules stipulates that a minimum of 40 square ft. of space be made available for each juvenile. There should be provision of free school education for the juveniles with medical and recreational facilities.

In the month of January of 1995,[18] when Ms. Mamta Sehgal Additional District & Sessions Judge visited an Observation Home for juvenile criminals at Magazine Road (Majnu Ka Tila) North

Delhi, she was simply shocked to see the horrible condition in the Observation Home. Rules were flouted with impunity. Young boys numbering 92 were herded like cattle inside two tiny rooms measuring 14 ft. × 10 ft. and 14 ft. × 25 ft. Thus each inmate had only 4.56 sq. ft. of space as against the requirement of 40 sq. ft. of the space.

Being a Member Secretary of the Delhi Legal and Advice Board, she moved the High Court seeking direction to the authorities of Delhi Administration to implement the Juvenile Justice Act and relevant Rules in their Observation Homes.

The escape of 72 inmates out of 105 from Majnu-Ka-Tila Observation Home in the month of November' 95 goes to prove that the authorities hardly moved in the interest of the juveniles who were young undertrials in the custody of the State.[18]

10.08 Rag-pickers

Rag-picking is an occupation primarily of migrant people of whom 30 per cent are women and 60 per cent are children. The job requires no skill, no education or training or any investment but brings them some 20 to 80 rupees per day. The duration of work are almost 8 hours per day. Rag-picking exposes them to many diseases, caused by microbes which act on the bio-degradable part of the garbage. Whereas conditions leading to manual rag-picking is a crime against humanity, a ban on rag-picking without making alternative arrangement is a crime against the society and the rag-pickers; as that will lead to starvation of those depending on earning by rag-picking.[19, 20]

10.09 Children as War Victims

Children are innocent guys and they should not be made to suffer on any account including wars between two countries or two factions. In ancient times, in the wars fought between two parties, only the fighting soldiers suffered. The civilians including women and children remained untouched. The classical example is of Ram-Ravan war fought on the soil of Lanka. Next great war of the ancient time was Mahabharat. In that also, the civil population in general remained untouched. Abhimanyu, the child warrior bravely fought the war but was killed by the combined attack of seven great warriors who had flouted all rules of war applicable in those days. Thereafter Aswathama did the heinous job of killing five Pandava children at night while they were sleeping. In so doing, he had stealthily sneaked into Pandava camp. These six were the only children who were victims of war.

Historically, the civil population including women and children were made to suffer by the Muslim invader, Nadirshah.

The 19th century had seen many wars being fought with guns. The 20th century has seen the development of a large number of long-range weapons and evolution of bomb culture. The war strategy has further been improved by introduction of germ warfare and use of nuclear weapons.

War and political upheavals have affected many countries and the vortex of violence is sucking in ever large number of children. The entire generations have grown up in the midst of brutal armed conflicts. By the end of the year 1995 conflicts have been in evidence in various countries—Angola, for over 30 years, Afghanistan for over 17 years, Sri-Lanka for 11 years and Somalia for 7 years.[21]

In the present day scenario, children have always been caught up in warfare and have to experience the same horrors as their parents. Children have suffered not only from bullets, bombs or mines or the death of their parents but also in the shape of exposure to violence and brutal deaths has emotionally affected generations of young people for their whole life. The figures for number of children affected on various counts as war victims are as under:[21]

1. Killed	2 millions
2. Disabled	4.5 millions
3. Rendered homeless	12 millions
4. Orphaned or separated from parents	Over one million
5. Psychologically traumatized	10 millions

10.10 Children as Soldiers

The recent development as regards the increasing use of children as soldiers is most deplorable. In twenty-five countries, children below 16 years of age have fought the war. The reasons contributing to the utilization of the children as soldiers are as under:[21]

(1) The present day Assault Rifle like AK-47 with its varianta and Americal M-16 are very simple to use. The AK-47 and its varianta can be stripped and reassembled even by a child aged 10 years.

(2) Children have another advantage for utilising their services as soldiers because they are easily intimidated and faithfully obey orders. They are less likely to run away and they do not demand salaries.
(3) Certain classes of children like, alone, orphaned, frightened, bored and frustrated choose to fight. A military unit for them would be serving as a kind of surrogate family.
(4) Children have also been recruited by force. Government and rebel in E1 Salvador, Ethiopia, Guatemala and Myanmer among others, have all conscripted children. The Renamo force in Mozambique have systematically practised forced recruitment. Renamo is estimated to have at least ten thousand soldiers, some as young as six years.
(5) The children may be subjected to terror and physical abuse in the belief that this will make them fierce warriors. In Sierra Leone in 1995, the Revolutionary United Front raided villages to capture children and force them to witness or take part in the torture and execution of their own relatives. Thus outlawed and brutalized, and often fed with crack or other drugs, the children were led to neighbouring villages to repeat the exercise.
(6) Children's acrual duties in warfare cover the whole range of military activities. At relatively quiet times in camp, this may be little more than cooking or carrying water they also serve as messengers or spies.

10.11 War Relief for Children

In addition to availability of adequate food and drink for children the undermentioned five tasks are to be taken up in respect of the problems of the those children who are victims of war:[21]

(1) The most urgent task for the children is attending to the needs of unaccompanied children and make them reunite children with their families. In the event of the family not being found, efforts should be made to find out fostering or adopting parents from the same cultural or ethinic group. Placing a child in the orphanage should be the last resort.
(2) *Demobilizing child soldiers:* Efforts should be made to rehabilitate child soldiers to their families and communities.
(3) *Healing the mental wounds*: Many child soldiers might have undergone horrifying experiences that will leave an impres-

sion on their mind for a pretty long time. Given the number of persons so affected, this task may seem daunting. Still much more has been learnt about how limited resources can be used to train local people who can then develop their own community-based approaches. In Rawanda in 1994–95, more than 2000 Rawandese were trained as counsellers and caregivers.

(4) *Restarting schools:* The collapse of the educational system is another disadvantage for the children. A good method of returning children to school is to restart education as soon as possible. For that purpose education can be started even in refugee camps. Attending classes, in whatever surroundings, can help the children to commence the process of recovery, healing and reconciliation.

(5) *Education for peace:* The children should be allowed to develop mutual understanding, to resolve differences without recourse to violence and to show how human diversity can be embraced rather than the basis for barbaric behaviours.

10.12 Conclusion

If children are to be loved and valued, the question is why they are used as fodder for the cannon. A weary response might lay the blame on innate human cruelty and duplicity. A cynic would also argue that our sensibilities and all conventions and declarations will inevitably crumble before the barrel of a gun.

UNICEF believes that the gap between rhetoric and reality represents a historic challenge. In response to so many destruction and pain, there have also been unprecedented efforts at peace-making and caring for the victims. The urgency now is to vastly enhance the means both to prevent future conflicts and to provide better support to the victims.[22]

REFERENCES

1. Section 361 of I.P.C. reads as under:

   "*361-Kidnapping from lawful guardianship*: Whoever takes or entices any minor under sixteen years of age, if a male, or under eighteen years of age if a female, or any person of unsound mind, out of the keeping of the lawful guardian of such minor or person of unsound mind, without the consent of such guardian, is said to kidnap such minot from lawful guardianship.

Explanation: The words "lawful guardian" in this Section include any person lawfully entrusted with the care or custody of such minor or other person.

Exception: This section does not extend to the act of any person who in good faith believes himself to be the father of an illegitimate child, or who, in good faith, believes himself to be entitled to the lawful custody of such child, unless such act is committed for an immoral or unlawful purpose."

Local Amendments

Manipur: In its application to the Union Territory of Manipur, in Section 361, for the word *"eighteen"* substitute the word *"fifteen"*.

2. Maulana Wahiuddin Khan, "Taking hostage is un-Islamic", *The Hindustan Times,* (Delhi Edn.) dated 15.3.1996.
3. Section 364-A I.P.C. reads as under:

   "364-A. Kidnapping for ransom, etc.: Whoever kidnaps or abducts any person or keeps a person in detention after such kidnapping or abduction, and threatens to cause death or hurt to such person, or by his conduct gives rise to a reasonable apprehension that such person may be put to death or hurt, or causes hurt or death to such person in order to compel the Government or any other person to do or abstain from doing any act or to pay ransom, shall be punishable with death, or imprisonment for life, and shall also be liable to fine."
4. Translated by U.S. Menon, "From Mangalam—A son sacrificed", *The Hindustan Times* (Delhi Edn.), dated 25.10.1987.
5. *Vijayalakshim* v. *State of Tamilnadu,* I(1993) CCR 451 (DB).
6. By arrangement with the Economist, "Where Death Squads the Street Children", *The Hindustan Times,* dated 5.8.1993 (Delhi Edn.).
7. By a Staff Reporter, "Child drowned by Father in Capital", Times of India (Delhi Edn.), dated 18.2.1996.
8. K. Kumar & Punam Rani, "Child Marriage as a Mode of Exploitation", Offences against Women (1996), Chapter 11, Regency Publications, New Delhi 110008.
9. H.T. Correspondent, "Students forced to change names", *The Hindustan Times* (Delhi Edn.) dated July 12, 1993.
10. Sec. 10 of the Act reads as under:

    10. Persons who may be adopted: No person shall be capable of being adopted unless the following conditions are fulfilled namely;

    (i) he or she is a Hindu;

    (ii) he or she has not already been adopted;

    (iii) he or she has not been married, unless there is a custom or usage applicable to the parties which permits who are married being taken in adoption;

    (iv) he or she has not completed the age of fifteen years, unless there is a custom usage applicable to the parties which permits persons who have completed the age of fifteen years being taken in adoption.
11. Section 11 of the Act reads as under:

    11. Other conditions for a valid adoption: In every adoption, the following conditions must be complied with:

    (i) if any adoption is of a son, the adoptive father or mother by whom the adoption is made must not have a Hindu son, son's son, or son's son's son (whether by legitimate blood relationship or by adoption), living at the time of adoption;

(ii) if the adoption is of a daughter, the adoptive father or mother by whom the adoption is made must not have a Hindu daughter, or son's daughter (whether by legitimate blood relationship or by adoption) living at the time of adoption;

(iii) if the adoption is by a male and the person to be adopted is a female, the adoptive father is at least twenty-one years older than the person to be adopted;

(iv) if the adoption is by a female and the person to be adopted is a male, the adoptive mother is at least twenty-one years older than the person to be adopted.

(v) the same child may not be adopted simultaneously by two or more persons;

(vi) the child to be adopted must be given and taken in adoption by the parents or guardian concerned or under their authority with intent to transfer the child from the family of its birth or in the case of an abandoned child or a child whose parentage is not known, from the place or family where it has been brought up to the family of its adoption;

Provided that the performance of *datta homan,* shall not be essential to the validity of an adoption.

12. Rangeen Singh "A Matter of Adoption", *The Hindustan Times* (Delhi Edn.), dated 16.12.1995.
13. Section 4 (a) of the Hindu Minority and Guardianship Act, 1956.
14. Sec. 7 of the Hindu Minority and Guardianship Act reads as under:-

    "7. *Natural guardianship of adopted son:* The natural guardianship of an adopted son who is a minor passes, on adoption, to the adoptive father and after him, to the adoptive mother."
15. Section 17 of the Hindu Minority and Guardianship Act, 1956 read with Section 7 of the Guardian and Wards Act, 1890.
16. Jaideep Sarin, "Seven-month old fights for her human rights", *The Hindustan Times,* (Delhi Edn.) dated 30.1.1996.
17. Lokpal Sethi, "Kid caught in complex Court-room drama", *The Hindustan Times* (Delhi Edn.) dated 27.2.1996."
18. From METRO CORRESPONDENT, "Where Reformation is needed", *The Hindustan Times* (Delhi Edn.) dated December 6, 1995.
19. H. T. Correspondent, "Ban on rag-picking may be hazardous", *The Hindustan Times,* (Delhi Edn.) dated 15.4.1995.
20. Sudhamahi Raghunathan, "Edging out rag-pickers", *The Hindustan Times* (Delhi Edn.) dated 15.6.1996.
21. Resource material, "Children in War", The State of the World's Children, UNICEF 1996, p. 13–20.
22. Resource material, The State of the World's Children, 1996 p. 10–11.

Chapter XI

POSTSCRIPT

11.01 Introduction

In the preceeding pages, topics which have direct bearing on crimes against children, have been discussed. It is proposed to present the left over matters which have not been included in the foregoing chapters. It is felt that without discussing these topics, proper justice to the subject matter of the book shall remain inconclusive. These, therefore, are presented in this Chapter.

11.02 Unfortunate Children

Stigma of illegitimacy

A child is born in consequence of sexual union between persons of opposite sex. If such persons are husband and wife declared through a wedlock, the child has the sanction of the society of legitimacy otherwise the child is illegitimate.

We all know that Karna of Mahabharata fame was a benevolent and a man of principle. He had all the virtues of a perfect personality and he was one among the best warriors of the time but on account of his parentage being unknown, he had to bear the brunt of illegitimacy for throughout his life although he was not at fault for anything.

The author (K.K.) vividly remembers one incident of his school days. A reputed semi-classical women singer of the town from the red-light area came to get her son admitted to a High School. While admitting him, the admission incharge smilingly enquired of her as to whose name be written in the column meant for 'Father'.

The women wittingly replied, "Sir, you record your own name against this column." It may not be out of place to mention that the boy, although an average student so far as studies were concerned, was excellent as a sportsman and always constituted the essential member of the school Eleven Football team.

This situation came up because the identity of a child is recognised through his/her father. An amendment in this procedure needs to be made that instead of the name of the father only, the name of either father or mother could be written. In the ancient times, a person used to be identified through both; that is; father and mother, for instance, Bhishma was called Ganga-putra, Yudhiśhthir, Bhim and Arjun as Kunti-putra and Duryodhan as Gandhari-putra. It would be appropriate in the present context as well, if a child is identified through mother also.

It is very embarrassing for a prostitute's child to receive education in a school as such children, even if they are promising as students and talented as a player, the stamp of illegitimacy gives him/her the sense of life-long inferiority complex.

Children of Divorced Parents

In a majority of cases, divorce result from conflict of ego between the spouse. The worst sufferer in that event is the minor child because of the deprivation of the love of one of the two, either father or mother. The next question which comes is about the guardianship of the boy. If this question is not settled by mutual consent, it will be decided within the framework of the applicable law, that is Section 6 of the Hindu Minority and Guardianship Act, 1956. This Section states that in the case of a boy or an unmarried girl, the father, and after him, the mother is the natural guardian of a Hindu minor. Proviso to this Section stipulates that the custody of a minor who has not completed the age of 5 years shall ordinarily be with the mother.

The child is, thus, placed in a very awkward situation particularly if the change of guard takes place at a later stage in life.

In case of conflict, the matter goes in litigation where the paramount consideration in this decision is the welfare of the minor as per Section 13 (1) of the Act. The litigation gets dragged into the Court for years together and the fate of the child continues to hang in balance.

The authors know a case where the divorce took place by mutual consent. The couple had a male child who was put in a far off place prestigious school and both father and mother used to visit the child in alternate months by turn. The child was unaware of the wrong that went with his parents. After he completed his school education and joined a college, he started living with his mother, who too, was a member of the teaching faculty in a University. It is at that stage that the boy came to know of the story of divorce between his father and mother. The boy after this became unusually grave and segregated himself from everybody.

Step-children

A step-child is the unwanted acquisition of one of the spouse and in most of the cases, the child gets indifferent treatment. However, in some cases, the step-child is welcomed by the step-father or step-mother.

11.03 Children with Problem of Learning Disability[1]

Dyslexia is a learning disability, the manifestation whereof could compare with the behaviour of a lazy child. How does then one support dyslexic child and motivate the lazy ones? One method is to include a dyslexic child for giving some concessions, like giving some extra time, use of a scribe and exemption from passing in the second language.

The next problem is to identify dyslexic children in order that the concession so given is not misused.

Dyslexia is essentially a language communication disorder. In the brain, there are language centres which identify symbols, interpret them, making them meaningful to the person in the form of language. The centre in a dyslexic child is not up to the mark. Further, the oxygen supply to this part of the brain also gets reduced due to its below par functioning. This results in inadequate blood supply. Thus, already a weak part gets weaker. The body system is so designed that instantaneously another part of the body takes up the functions of the impaired part. But, this part is not designed to do so and is less defective. Hénce, the disability in a dyslexic child.

The disability manifests itself through poor handwriting, slow reading, confusion over similar looking words and even bad copying from black-boards. The dyslexic student, however grasps quickly. He is even quicker with the reply and understands concepts in a stein. Of course, one must be wary, and not look for an explanation in dyslexic for the poor performance of a normal child. It is only the in-depth familiarity with the problem that will help clarify the nature of disability.

Symptoms

(1) Better comprehension than reading or writing skills.
(2) Is not able to read words properly in order or with the right emphasis.
(3) Reads backward of jumbles up the letters of a word.
(4) Copies badly from black-boards.
(5) The subject could be a left-hander and more often a male child.

11.04 Handling Adolescents[2]

A child learns to live and grows to become an individual under the care, protection and guidance of parents, guardians and teachers. It is only when they step out of adolescence that they enter into a world outside on their own, away from the safe keeping of elders. This is the second phase of life as the teenager has to become an adult and survive like that.

The adolescents are filled with zest and enthusiasm for trying out their wits against the whole world. Often they think they can reform the evils that has over-taken the society. They do not foresee the problems which is in store for them.

In order that an adolescent does not get astray and entrapped into bad habits like drug-abuse, sex-indulgence etc., a parent is required to give a lot of love and reasonable support to their children required to make them feel secure. This however, should not go beyond a certain limit to the extent of getting spoilt.

What the parents should do?

(1) Guide the adolescent to develop a strong mind and the ability to surmount all temptation and a strength of character in order to enable them to face all eventualities of life, if necessary, by openly and frankly discussing the prons and cons of life.
(2) Often parents and children, owing presumably due to 'generation gap', seem to be in rival camps leading to a split. It is for

the parents to try to fill up this generation gap. The parents therefore, should behave like friends, after a certain age.

(3) Adolescents should also be infused with values, control and discipline that sustains them against the tumultous holes and formenting ebb and flow of traumas. The capacity of making a distinction between good and bad and an honesty inherent in the mind can guide adolescents and even help the country to be free from the disease of corruption that is eating into the vitality of the nation.

(4) Adolescents be given the right perspective and balanced attitudes to make them confident by believing in themselves and correctly appraise their own capabilities. They should acquire self-esteem devoid of any complex and need to learn the ability to accept challenges and face courageously in order to be able to in the control of situations as and when required.

(5) An adolescent with proper training backed by parental love and support cannot falter or succumb easily to whatever temptations are in store.

(6) Life is full of seen and unseen problems and the only way out is to fortify children to face realities of life with integrity, fortitude, patience and courage so that they never buckle under any pressure whatever.

11.05 Education on AIDS Awareness[3]

The spread of AIDS virus is a major hitherto unknown factor in predicting social trends, particularly as they affect younger generation.

In addition to acquisition of AIDS virus by birth, AIDS do spread on account of multiple sex activities and adolescents fall a prey to it owing to a lack of knowledge. Education is needed to provide them with authentic knowledge as regards their critical concerns with a view to inculcating in them a rational attitude to awards sex, phenomena of HIV/AIDS and drug-abuse and developing in them respect for opposite sex and responsible behaviour towards sex and drugs.

The present conceptualisation of adolescent education in the context of Indian socio-cultural milieu has deliberately avoided another basic assumption which forms the basis of sex-education programme in many other societies.

Since the adolescents are likely to enter into hetero-sexual and homo-sexual relationships and there is growing incidence of pre-marital pregnancies, unwed motherhood and adolescent sex-crimes, the adolescents should be imparted knowledge about sex and sexuality, so that they can practice safe sex and develop assertive to say 'no' to sex.

The concept of adolescent education may be viewed as a very broad educational endeavour that may focus on a number of critical concerns of adolescents which are closely inter-related to sex-education.

The objectives of the adolescent education should aim at:

(1) to provide authentic information and to develop among students proper understanding of the process of growing up;
(2) to promote among them healthy attitude towards sex and responsible behaviour towards the opposite sex in consonance with the varied socio-cultural needs of sexual morality;
(3) to make them aware of the physiological, psychological, socio-cultural and interpersonal issues relating to the period of adolescence;
(4) to help them understand the implications of AIDS and the causes and consequences of HIV, infections as well as the ways and means to avoid such infection; and
(5) to make them aware of the factors leading to drug-abuse, its consequences and ways of preventing drug-abuse and the development of an attitude to say 'no' to proposals to drug use.

In a seminar organised by the National Council of Education, Research and Training (NCERT), the following strategies were considered useful:

(1) Conducting needs information studies of the problem of adolescents belonging to different cultural settings;
(2) Preparation of conceptual framework of adolescence education on the basis of a status study to be conducted for identification of suitable entry points in the existing curriculum;
(3) Preparation of materials on adolescence education for different target groups;
(4) Integration of elements of adolescence education in the courses of pre-service and in-service teachers education;
(5) Integration of elements of adolescence education in syllabi and text-books;

(6) Intensive orientation of curriculum framers, text-book authors, teachers, parents and educational administrators; and
(7) Promotion of students' activity even before the elements are integrated in schools syllabi and text-books.

11.06 Rearing up Children in Right Perspective[4]

It is very difficult and expensive to rear a child today amidst the glamour of toys, cartoons, video games, birth-day parties and designer clothes which a child must be provided to compete with acquisition of similar articles by the child of a neighbour or the child in a family where the parents visit. The present generation parents may put a question to their parents as to how they were able to bring up 3-4 children with comparatively lower income? Surely the answer would be that the times were different. There were no ice-cream parlours selling 100 odd flavour in a scoop for sixty ruppees, no designer boutiques for children where a pair of jeans would cost Rs one thousand or so and no toy shops where a child could pick up a PC or an electronic calculator for a few thousand of rupees.

The most eager consumers of everything from a bottle of Pepsi to a washing machine are children and advertisements through TV very easily attract the attention of children most of the time. Can one, in these circumstances raise sensible, well-behaved, non-acquisitive children with a healthy respect for hard earned money?

Sorting out these weighty problems—trying for a balance between disciplining a child and giving free rein to his natural high spirits, teaching him not to take many things not very essential and yet trying to inculcate sensitivity and consideration is a difficult enough battle without the added glamour of Television, toys, peer group pressure and the lot. In this situation, one should have fun with his kids, bring them up the way which comes most naturally and through the process of wait and watch. If one is okay, the child is likely to be okay.

11.07 Population Galore

India attained independence in the year 1947 and since then five census in the years 1951, 1961, 1971, 1981 and 1991 have been held. The population of this country which was recorded at 361 millions in 1951 during the first census, rose to, 439 millions in 1961, 541 millions in 1971, 683 millions in 1981 and 844 millions in 1991. It further rose to 879. 5 millions in 1992 and 883 millions in 1993,[5] and by the time the book is published in 1996, it will exceed 900 million mark.

With this increase in population, the country is faced with enormous problems in all spheres, that is; food, drink, electricity, housing, education, transport, health and employment. The present population is nothing but a mighty and mammoth mass of humanity and any further growth is fraught with insurmountable problems. It is not only harmful to the nation but also to the individual and the would be citizens of the country. The problems raised by the people is for the people and will harm the people and could be solved by the people only. The only solution to this problem essentially lies in achieving a 'Zero' growth tare.

11.08 Children in the 21st Century

It was in the year 1980, the UNICEF launched the child survival and development revolution which saved more than 12 million children by the end of the decade.

With the 1990s, a new era has opened up for children with the world making great strides towards achieving the World Summit for children's basic health, nutrition and education goals for the year 2000 and a campaign that has brought universal ratification of the Convention on the Rights of the child nearly within reach. Looking towards the year 2000 and beyond, children are increasingly at the centre of the International Human Rights and development agenda and despite the depredations of war and poverty, global progress is possible.[6]

As we come to the end of the century, the education of children has become one of the centre-pieces of International development. The International community has been so united on the issue on the priority for Universal education.

This is precisely what makes the future of children a realm of optimism and in spite of war and poverty the world will not abandon, marginalize or deprecate children.

Fifty years of efforts, beginning from 1946 by the UNICEF has put children at the centre of the International Development and Human Right Agenda. It is possible to say, even amid the horrors of conflict and deprivation that the 21st century will belong to the children.[7]

REFERENCES

1. Sudhamahi Raghunathan "Coping with Dyslexia", *The Hindustan Times,* (Delhi Edn.) dated 24.2.1996.
2. Rangeen Singh, "It's a tough life", *The Hindustan Times* (Delhi Edn.) dated 27.1.1996.
3. Uma Nair, "New generation at Risk", *The Hindustan Times,* (Delhi Edition) dated 20.1.1996
4. Poonam Saxena, "Bringing up the Baba Log", *The Hindustan Times, (Delhi* Edn.*) dated* 13.2.1996.
5. Mangu Ram Gupta, "Sad, Sordid Scenario", *The Hindustan Times,* (Delhi Edn.) dated 1.7.1993.
6. From Historical Record of Maggie Black on UNICEF (Past and Present), UNICEF, Oxford University Press 1996, cited in Chapter II in the details of contents, Chapter II of the State of the World's Children (1996).
7. Social goals: 1995 and 2000, *"The State of the World's Children, 1996, Published by UNICEF"*, Oxford University Press, p. 73.

ANNEXURE

CONVENTION ON THE RIGHTS OF CHILD

(Adopted by the General Assembly of the United Nations on 20th November 1989)

Preamble

The States Parties to the present Convention: Considering that, in accordance with the principles proclaimed in the Charter of the United Nations, recognition of the inherent dignity and of the equal and inalienable rights of all members of the human family is the foundation of freedom, justice and peace in the world.

Bearing in mind that the peoples of the United Nations have, in the Charter, reaffirmed their faith in fundamental human rights and in the dignity and worth of the human person, and have determined to promote social progress and better standards of life in larger freedom.

Recognizing that the United Nations has, in the Universal Declaration of Human Rights and in the International Convenants on Human Rights, proclaimed and agreed that everyone is entitled to all the rights and freedoms set forth therein, without distinction of any kind, such as race, colour, sex, language, religion, political or other opinion, national or social origin, property, birth or other status.

Recalling that, in the Universal Declaration of Human Rights, the United Nations has proclaimed that *childhood is entitled to special care and assistance.*

Convinced that the family, as the fundamental group of society and the natural environment for the growth and well-being of all its members and particularly *children, should be afforded the necessary protection and assistance* so that it can fully assume its responsibilities within the community.

Recognizing that *the child,* for the full and harmonious development of his or her personality, *should grow up in a family environment, in an atmosphere of happiness, love and understanding.*

Considering that *the child should be fully prepared to live an individual life in society, and brought up in the spirit of ideals* proclaimed in the Charter of the United Nations, and in particular in the spirit of peace, dignity, tolerance, freedom, equality and solidarity.

Bearing in mind that the *need to extend particular care to the child* has been stated in the Geneva declaration of the Rights of the Child, of 1924 and in the Declaration of the Rights of the Child adopted by the General Assembly on 20th November of 1959 and recognized in the Universal Declaration of Human Rights, in the International Convenant on Civil and Political Rights (in particular in Articles 23 and 24), in the International Convenant on Economic, Social and Cultural Rights (in particular in Article 10) and in the Statutes and in the relevant instruments of specialized agencies and International organizations concerned with the *welfare of the children.*

Bearing in mind that, as indicated in the Declaration of the Rights of the Child, *"The Child,* by reason of his physical and mental immaturity, *needs special safeguards and care, including appropriate legal protection, before, as well as after birth."*

Recalling the provisions of the Declaration on social and legal principles relating to the *Protection and Welfare of Children, with Special Reference to Foster Placement and Adoption Nationally* and *Internationally;* the United Nations Standard Minimum Rules for the Administration of Juvenile Justice (the Beijing Rules); and the Declaration on the Protection of Women and Children in Emergency and Armed Conflict.

Recognizing that, in all countries in the world, there are *children living in exceptionally difficult* condition, and that such children need special consideration.

Taking due account of the importance of the traditions and cultural values of each people for the *protection and harmonious development of the child.*

Recognizing the importance of International co-operation for improving the living conditions of children in every country, in particular in the developing countries,

Have Agreed as Follows:

PART I

Article 1: For the purposes of the present Convention, a child means every human being below the age of eighteen years unless, under the law applicable to the child, majority is attained earlier.

Article 2: (1) States Parties shall respect and ensure the rights set forth in the present Convention to each child within their jurisdiction without discrimination of any kind, irrespective of the child's or his or her parent's or legal guardian's race, colour, sex, language, religion, political or other opinion, national, ethnic or social origin, property, disability, birth or other status.

(2) States parties shall take all appropriate measures to ensure that the child is protected against all forms of discrimination or punishment on the basis of the status, activities, expressed opinions, or beliefs of the child's parents, legal guardians of family members.

Article 3: (1) In all actions concerning children, whether undertaken by public or private social welfare institutions, courts of law, administrative authorities or legislative bodies, the best interests of the child shall be a primary consideration.

(2) States Parties undertake to ensure the child such protection and care as is necessary for his or her well-being, taking into account the rights and duties of his or her parents, legal guardians, or other individuals legally responsible for him or her, and, to this end, shall take all appropriate legislative and administrative measures.

(3) States Parties shall ensure that the institutions, services and facilities responsible for the care or protection of children shall conform with the standards established by competent authorities, particularly in the areas of safety, health, in the number and suitability of their staff, as well as competent supervision.

Article 4: States Parties shall undertake all appropriate legislative, administrative, and other measures for the implementation of the rights recognised in the present convention. With regards to economic, social and cultural rights, State Parties shall undertake such measures to the maximum extent of their available resources and, where needed, within the framework of international co-operation.

Article 5: States Parties shall respect the responsibilities, rights and duties of parents or where applicable, the members of the extended family or community as provided for by local custom, legal guardians or other persons legally responsible for the child, appropriate direction and guidance in the exercise by the child of the rights recognized in the present Convention.

Article 6: (1) States Parties recognize that every child has the right to life.

(2) States Parties shall ensure to the maximum extent possible the survival and development of the child.

Article 7: (1) The child shall be registered immediately after birth and shall have the right from birth to a name, the right to acquire a nationality and as far as possible, the right to know and be cared for by his or her parents.

(2) States Parties shall ensure the implementation of these rights in accordance with their national law and their obligations under the relevant international instruments in this field, in particular where the child would otherwise be Stateless.

Article 8: (1) States Parties undertake to respect the right of the child to preserve his or her identity including nationality, name and family relations as recognised by law without unlawful interference.

(2) Where a child is illegally deprived of some or all of the elements of his or her identity. States Parties shall provide appropriate assistance and protection, with a view to speedily re-establishing his or her identity.

Article 9: (1) States Parties shall ensure that a child shall not be separated from his or her parents against their will, except when competent authorities subject to judicial review determine, in accordance with applicable law and procedures, that such separation is necessary for the best interests of the child. Such determination may be necessary in a particular case such as one involving abuse or neglect of the child by the parents, or one where the parents are living separately and a decision must be made as to the child's place of residence.

(2) In any proceedings pursuant to paragraph (1) of the present article, all interested parties shall be given an opportunity to participate in the proceedings and make their views known.

(3) States Parties shall respect the right of the child who is separated from one or both parents to maintain personal relations and direct contact with both parents on a regular basis except if it is contrary to the child's best interests.

(4) Where such separation results from any action initiated by a State Party, such as the detention, imprisonment, exile, deportation or death (including death arising from any cause while the person is in the custody of the State) of one or both parents or of the child, that State Party shall, upon request, provide the parents, the child or, if appropriate, another member of the family with the essential information concerning the whereabouts of the absent member(s) of the family unless the provision of the information would be detrimental to the well-being of the child. States Parties shall further ensure that the submission of such request shall of itself entail no adverse consequences for the person(s) concerned.

Article 10: (1) In accordance with the obligation of States Parties under Article 9, paragraph 1, applications by a child or his or her parents to enter or leave a State Party for the purpose of family reunification shall be dealt with by States Parties in a positive, humane and expeditious manner. States Parties shall further ensure that the submission of such a request shall entail no adverse consequences for the applicants and for the members of their family.

(2) A child whose parents reside in different States shall have the right to maintain on a regular basis, save in exceptional circumstances personal relations and direct contacts with both parents. Towards that end and in accordance with the obligation of States Parties under Article 9, Paragraph 1, States Parties shall respect the right of the child and his or her parents to leave any country, including their own, and to enter their own country. The right to leave any country shall be subject only to such restrictions as are prescribed by law and which are necessary to protect the national security, public order (*ordre public*), public health or morals or the rights and freedoms of others and are consistent with the other rights recognized in the present Convention.

Article 11: (1) State Parties shall take measures to combat the illicit transfer and non-return of children abroad.

(2) To this end, States Parties shall promote the conclusion of bilateral or multilateral agreements or accession to existing agreements.

Article 12: (1) States Parties shall assure to the child who is capable of forming his or her own views the right to express those views freely in all matters affecting the child, the views of the child being given due weight in accordance with the age and maturity of the child.

(2) For this purpose, the child shall in particular be provided the opportunity to be heard in any judicial and administrative proceedings affecting the child, either directly, or through a representative or an appropriate body, in a manner consistent with the procedural rules of national law.

Article 13: (1) The child shall have the right to freedom of expression; this right shall include freedom to seek, receive and impart information and ideas of all kinds, regardless of frontiers, either orally, in writing or in print, in the form of art, or through any other media of the child's choice.

(2) The exercise of this right may be subject to certain restrictions, but these shall only be such as are provided by law and are necessary:

(a) For respect of the rights or reputations of others; or

(b) For the protection of national security or of public order (*ordre public*), or of public health or morals.

Article 14: (1) States Parties shall respect the right of the child to freedom of thought, conscience and religion.

(2) States Parties shall respect the rights and duties of the parents and, when applicable, legal guardians, to provide direction to the child in the exercise of his or her right in a manner consistent with the evolving capacities of the child.

(3) Freedom to manifest one's religion or beliefs may be subject only to such limitations as are prescribed by law and are necessary to protect public safety, order, health or morals, or the fundamental rights and freedoms of others.

Article 15: (1) States Parties recognize the rights of the child to freedom of association and to freedom of peaceful assembly.

(2) No restrictions may be placed on the exercise of these rights other than those imposed in conformity with the law and which are necessary in a democratic society in the interests of national security or public safety, public order (*ordre public*), the protection

of public health or morals or the protection of the rights and freedoms of others.

Article 16: (1) No child shall be subject to arbitrary or unlawful interference with his or her privacy, family, home or correspondence, nor, to unlawful attacks on his or her honor and reputation.

(2) The child has the right to the protection of the law against such interference or attacks.

Article 17: States Parties recognize the important function performed by the mass media and shall ensure that the child has access to information and material from a diversity of national and informational sources, especially those aimed at the promotion of his or her social, spiritual and moral well-being and physical and mental health. To this end, States Parties shall:

(a) Encourage the mass media to disseminate information and material of social and cultural benefit to the child and in accordance with the spirit of Article 29.

(b) Encourage international co-operation in the production, exchange and dissemination of such information and material from a diversity of cultural, national and international sources.

(c) Encourage the production and dissemination of children's books.

(d) Encourage the mass media to have particular regard to the linguistic needs of the child who belongs to a minority group or who is indigenous.

(e) Encourage the development of appropriate guidelines for the protection of the child from information and material injurious to his or her well-being, bearing in mind the provisions of Articles 13 and 18.

Article 18: (1) States Parties shall use their best efforts to ensure recognition of the principle that both parents have common responsibilities for the upbringing and development of the child. Parents or, as the case may be, legal guardians, have the primary responsibility for the upbringing and development of the child. The best interests of the child will be their basic concern.

(2) For the purpose of guaranteeing and promoting the rights set forth in the present Convention, State Parties shall render appropriate assistance to parents and legal guardians in the performance of their child rearing responsibilities and shall ensure the development of institutions, facilities and services to the care of children.

(3) States Parties shall take all appropriate measures to ensure that children of working parents have the right to benefit from child care services and facilities for which they are eligible.

Article 19: (1) States Parties shall take all appropriate legislative, administrative, social and educational measures to protect the child from all forms of physical or mental violence, injury or abuse, neglect or negligent treatment, maltreatment or exploitation, including sexual abuse, while in the care of parent(s), legal guardian(s) or any other person who has the care of the child.

(2) Such protective measures should, as appropriate include effective procedures for the establishment of social programmes to provide necessary support for the child and for those who have the care of the child, as well as for other forms of prevention and for identification, reporting, referral, investigation, treatment and follow-up of instances of child maltreatment described heretofore, and as appropriate, for judicial involvement.

Article 20: (1) A child temporarily or permanently deprived of his or her family environment, or in whose own best interests cannot be allowed to remain in that environment, shall be entitled to special protection and assistance provided by the State.

(2) States Parties shall, in accordance with their national laws ensure alternative care for such a child.

(3) Such care could include, *inter-alia*, foster placement, *kafala* of Inslamic Law, adoption or if necessary placement in suitable institutions for the care of children. When considering solutions, due regard shall be paid to the desirability of continuity in a child's upbringing and to the child's ethnic, religious, cultural and linguistic background.

Article 21: States Parties that reconize and/or permit the system of adoption shall ensure that the best interests of the child shall be the paramount consideration and they shall:

(a) Ensure that the adoption of a child is authorized only by competent authorities who determine, in accordance with applicable law and procedures and on the basis of all pertinent and reliable information, that the adoption is permissible in view of the child's status concerning parents, relatives and legal guardians and that, if required, the persons concerned have given their informed consent to the adoption on the basis of such counselling as may be necessary.

(b) Recognize that the inter-country adoption may be considered as an alternative means of child's care, if the child cannot be placed in a foster or an adoptive family or cannot in any suitable manner be cared for in the child's country of origin.

(c) Ensure that the child concerned by inter-country adoption enjoys safeguards and standards equivalent to those existing in the case of national adoption.

(d) Take all appropriate measures to ensure that, in intercountry adoption, the placement does not result in improper financial gain for those involved in it.

(e) Promote, where appropriate, the objectives of the present article by concluding bilateral or multilateral arrangements or agreements, and endeavour, within this framework, to ensure that the placement of the child in another country is carried out by competent authorities or organs.

Article 22: (1) States Parties shall take appropriate measures to ensure that a child who is seeking refugee status or who is considered a refugee in accordance with applicable international or domestic law and procedures shall, whether unaccompanied or accompanied by his or her parents or by any other person, receive appropriate protection and humanitarian assistance in the enjoyment of applicable rights set forth in the present Convention and in other International human rights of humanitarian instruments to which the said States are parties.

(2) For this purpose, States Parties shall provide as they consider appropriate, co-operation in any efforts by the United Nations and other competent intergovernmental organizations or non-governmental organizations co-operating with the United Nations to protect and assist such a child and to trace the parents or other members of the family of any refugee child in order to obtain information necessary for reunification with his or her family. In cases where no parents or other members of the family can be found, the child shall be accorded the same protection as any other child permanently or temporarily deprived of his or family environment for any reason, as set forth in the present Convention.

Article 23: (1) States Parties recognize that a mentally or physically disabled child should enjoy a full and decent life, in conditions which ensure dignity, promote self-reliance and facilitate the child's active participation in the community.

(2) States Parties recognize the right of the disabled child to special care and shall encourage and ensure the extension, subject to available resources, to the eligible child and those responsible for

his or her care, of assistance for which application is made and which is appropriate to the child's condition and to the circumstances of the parents or others caring for the child.

(3) Recognizing the special needs of a disabled child, assistance extended in accordance with Paragraph 2 of the present Article shall be provided free of charge, whenever possible, taking into account the financial resources of the parents or others caring for the child, and shall be designed to ensure that the disabled child has effective access to and receives education, training, health services, rehabilitation services, preparation for employment and recreation opportunities in a manner conducive to the child's achieving the fullest possible social integration and individual development, including his or her cultural and spiritual development.

(4) States Parties shall promote, in the spirit of international cooperation, the exchange of appropriate information in the field of preventive health care and of medical, psychological and functional treatment of disabled children, including dissemination of and access to information concerning methods of rehabilitation, education and vocational services, with the aim of enabling States Parties to improve their capabilities and skills and to widen their experience in these areas. In this regard, particular account shall be taken of the needs of developing countries.

Article 24: (1) State Parties recognize the right of the child to the enjoyment of the highest attainable standard of health and to facilitate for the treatment of illness and rehabilitation of health. States Parties shall strive to ensure that no child is deprived of his or her right of access to such health care services.

(2) States Parties shall pursue full implementation of this right and, in particular, shall take appropriate measures:

(a) to diminish infant and child mortality;

(b) to ensure the provision of necessary medical assistance and health care to all children with emphasis on the development of primary health care;

(c) to combat disease and malnutrition, including within the framework of primary health care, *inter alia*, the application of readily available technology and through the provision of adequate nutritious foods and clean drinking water, taking into consideration the dangers and risks of environmental pollution;

(d) to ensure appropriate pre-natal and post-natal health care for mothers;

(e) to ensure that all segments of society, in particular parents and children, are informed, have access to education and are supported in the use of basic knowledge of child health and nutrition, the advantage of breast feeding, hygiene and environmental sanitation and the prevention of accidents;

(f) to develop preventive health care, guidance for parents and family planning, education and services.

(3) States Parties shall take all effective and appropriate measures with a view to abolishing traditional practices prejudicial to the health of children.

(4) States Parties undertake to promote and encourage international co-operation with a view to achieving progressively the full realization of the right recognized in the present Article. In this regard, particular account shall be taken of the needs of developing countries.

Article 25: States Parties recognize the right of a child who has been placed by the competent authorities for the purposes of care, protection or treatment of his or her physical or mental health to a periodic review of the treatment provided to the child and all other circumstances relevant to his or her placement.

Article 26: (1) States Parties shall recognize for every child the right to benefit from social security, including social insurance, and shall take the necessary measures to achieve the full realization of this right in accordance with their national law.

(2) The benefits should, where appropriate, be granted, taking into account the resources and the circumstances of the child and persons having responsibility for the maintenance of the child, as well as any other consideration relevant to an application for benefits made by or on behalf of the child.

Article 27: (1) States Parties recognize the right of every child to a standard of living adequate for the child's physical, mental, spiritual, moral and social development.

(2) The parent(s) or others responsible for the child have the primary responsibility to secure, within their abilities and financial capacities, the conditions of living necessary for the child's development.

(3) States Parties, in accordance with national conditions and within their means, shall take appropriate measures to assist parents

and others responsible for the child to implement this right and shall, in case of need, provide material assistance and support programmes particularly with regard to nutrition, clothing and housing.

(4) States Parties shall take all appropriate measures to secure the recovery of maintenance for the child from the parents or other persons having financial responsibility for the child both within the State Party and from abroad. In particular, where the person having financial responsibility for the child lives in a state different from that of the child, States Parties shall promote the accession to International agreements or the conclusion of such agreements, as well as the making of other appropriate arrangements.

Article 28: (1) States Parties recognize the right of the child to education, and with a view to achieving this right progressively and on the basis of equal opportunity, they shall, in particular:

(a) make primary education compulsory and available free to all;

(b) encourage the development of different forms of secondary education, including general and vocational education, make them available and accessible to every child and take appropriate measures such as the introduction of free education and offering financial assistance in case of need;

(c) make higher education accessible to all on the basis of capacity by every appropriate means;

(d) make educational and vocational information and guidance available and accessible to all children;

(e) take measures to encourage regular attendance at schools and the reduction of drop-out rates.

(2) States Parties shall take all appropriate measures to ensure that school discipline is administered in a manner consistent with the child's human dignity and in conformity with the present Convention.

(3) States Parties shall promote and encourage international cooperation in matters relating to education, in particular with a view to contributing to the elimination of ignorance and illiteracy throughout the world and facilitating access to scientific and technical knowledge and modern teaching methods. In this regard, particular account shall be taken of the needs of developing countries.

Article 29: (1) States Parties agree that the education of the child shall be directed to:

(a) the development of the child's personality, talents and mental and physical abilities to their fullest potential;

(b) the development of respect for human rights and fundamental freedoms, and for the principles enshrined in the charter of the United Nations;

(c) the development of respect for the child's parents, his or her own cultural identity, language and values of the country in which the child is living, the country from which he or she may originate, and for civilizations different from his or her own;

(d) the preparation of the child for responsible life in a free society, in the spirit of understanding, peace, tolerance, equality of sexes and friendship among all peoples, ethnic, national and religious groups and persons of indigenous origin;

(e) the development of respect for the natural environment.

(2) No part of the present Article or Article 28 shall be construed so as to interfere with the liberty of individuals and bodies to establish and direct educational institutions, subject always to the observance of the principles set forth in Paragraph 1 of the present Article and to the requirements that the education given in such institutions shall conform to such minimum standards as may be laid down by the State.

Article 30: In those States in which ethnic, religious or linguistic minorities or persons of indigenous origin exist, a child belonging to such a minority or who is indigenous shall not be denied the right, in community with other members of his or her group, to enjoy his or her own culture, to profess and practise his or her own religion, or to use his or her own language.

Article 31: (1) States Parties recognize the right of the child to rest and leisure, to engage in play and recreational activities appropriate to the age of the child and to participate freely in cultural life and the arts.

(2) States Parties shall respect and promote the right of the child to participate fully in cultural and artistic life and shall encourage the provision of appropriate and equal opportunities for cultural, artistic, recreational and leisure activity.

Article 32: (1) States Parties recognize the right of the child to be protected from economic exploitation and from performing any work that is likely to be hazardous or to interfere with the child's education, or to be harmful to the child's health or physical, mental, spiritual, moral or social development.

(2) States Parties shall take legislative, administrative, social and educational measures to ensure the implementation of the present Article. To this end, and having regard to the relevant provisions of other International Instruments, States Parties shall in particular;

(a) provide for a minimum age or minimum ages for admission to employment;

(b) provide for appropriate regulation of the hours and conditions of employment;

(c) provide for appropriate penalties or other sanctions to ensure the effective enforcement of the present Article.

Article 33: States Parties shall take all appropriate measures, including legislative, administrative, social and educational measure, to protect children from the illicit use of narcotic drugs and psychotropic substances as defined in the relevant international treaties, and to prevent the use of children in the illicit production and trafficking of such substances.

Article 34: States Parties undertake to protect the child from all forms of sexual exploitation and sexual abuse. For these purposes, States Parties shall in particular take all appropriate national, bilateral and multilateral measures to prevent:

(a) the inducement of coercion of a child to engage in any unlawful sexual activity;

(b) the exploitative use of children in prostitution or other unlawful sexual practices;

(c) the exploitative use of children in pornographic performances and materials.

Article 35: States Parties shall take all appropriate national, bilateral and multilateral measures to prevent the abduction of the sale of or traffic in children for any purpose or in any form.

Article 36: States Parties shall protect the child against all other forms of exploitation prejudicial to any aspects of the child's welfare.

Article 37: States Parties shall ensure that:

(a) No child shall be subjected to torture or other cruel, inhuman or degrading treatment or punishment. Neither capital punishment nor life imprisonment without possibility of release shall be imposed for offenses committed by persons below eighteen years of age.

(b) No child shall be deprived of his or her liberty unlawfully or arbitrarily. The arrest, detention or imprisonment of a child shall be in conformity with the law and shall be used only as a measure of last resort and for the shortest appropriate period of time;

(c) Every child deprived of liberty shall be treated with humanity and respect for the inherent dignity of the human person, and in a manner which takes into account the needs of persons of his or her age. In particular, every child deprived of liberty shall be separated from adults unless it is considered in the child's best interest not to do so and shall have the right to maintain contact with his or her family through correspondence and visits, save in exceptional circumstances;

(d) Every child deprived of his or her liberty shall have the right to prompt access to legal and other appropriate assistance, as well as the right to challenge the legality of the deprivation of his or her liberty before a Court or other competent, independent and impartial authority, and to a prompt decision on any such action.

Article 38: (1) States Parties undertake to respect and to ensure respect for rules of International Humanitarian Law applicable to them in armed conflicts which are relevant to the child.

(2) States Parties shall take all feasible measures to ensure that persons who have not attained the age of fifteen years do not take a direct part in hostilities.

(3) States parties shall refrain from recruiting any person who has not attained the age of fifteen years into their armed forces. In recruiting among those persons who have attained the age of fifteen years but who have not attained the age of eighteen years, States Parties shall endeavour to give priority to those who are oldest.

(4) In accordance with their obligations under International Humanitarian Law to protect the civilian population in armed conflicts, States Parties shall take all feasible measures to ensure protection and care of children who are affected by an armed conflict.

Article 39: States Parties shall take all appropriate measures to promote physical and psychological recovery and social re-integration of a child victim of any form of neglect, exploitation, or abuse, torture or any other form of cruel, inhuman or degrading treatment of punishment, or armed conflicts. Such recovery and re-integration shall take place in an environment which fosters the health, self-respect and dignity of the child.

Article 40: (1) States Parties recognize the right of every child alleged as, accused of, or recognized as having infringed the penal law to be treated in a manner consistent with the promotion of the child's sense of dignity and worth, which reinforces the child's respect for the human rights and fundamental freedoms of others and which takes into account the child's age and desirability of promoting the child's re-integration and the child's assuming a constructive role in society.

(2) To this end, and having regard to the relevant provisions of Instrumental Instruments, States Parties shall, in particular, ensure that;

(a) No child shall be alleged as, accused of, or recognized as having infringed the penal law by reason of acts of ommissions that were not prohibited by national or international law at the time they were committed.

(b) Every child alleged as or accused of having infringed the penal law has at least the following guarantees;

(i) To be presumed innocent unit proven guilty according to law;

(ii) To be informed promptly and directly of the charges against him or her, and, if appropriate, through his or her parents or legal guardians, and to have legal or other appropriate assistance in the preparation and presentation of his or her defence;

(iii) To have the matter determined without delay by a competent, independent and impartial authority or judicial body in a fair hearing according to law, in the presence of legal or other appropriate assistance and, unless it is considered not to be in the best interest of the child, in particular, taking into account his or her age or situation, his or her parents or legal guardians;

(iv) Not to be compelled to give testimony or to confess guilt; to examine or have examined adverse witnesses and to obtain the participation and examination under conditions of equality;

(v) If considered to have infringed the penal law, to have this decision and any measures imposed in consequence thereof reviewed by a higher competent, independent and impartial authority or judicial body according to law;

(vi) To have the free assistance of an interpreter if the child cannot understand or speak the language used;

(vii) To have his or her privacy fully respected at all stages of the proceedings.

(3) States Parties shall seek to promote the establishment of laws, procedures, authorities and institutions specifically applicable to children alleged as, accused of, or recognized as having infringed the penal law, and, in particular;

(a) the establishment of a minimum age below which children shall be presumed not to have the capacity to infringe the penal law;

(b) whenever appropriate and desirable, measures for dealing with such children without resorting to judicial proceedings, providing that human rights and legal safeguards are fully respected.

(4) A variety of dispositions, such as care, guidance and supervision orders; counselling; probation; foster care; education and vocational training programmes and other alternatives to institutional care shall be available to ensure that children are dealt with in a manner appropriate to their well-being and proportionate both to their circumstances and the offence.

Article 41: Nothing in the present Convention shall afiect any provisions which are more conducive to the realization of the rights of the child and which may be contained in;

(a) The law of a State Party; or

(b) International law in force for that State;

PART II

Article 42: States Parties undertake to make the principles and provisions of the Convention widely known, by appropriate and active means, to adults and children alike.

Article 43: (1) For the purpose of examining the progress made by States Parties in achieving the realization of the obligations undertaken in the present Convention, there shall be established a Committee on the Rights of the child which shall carry out the functions hereinafter provided.

(2) The Committee shall consist of ten experts of high moral standing and recognized competence in the field covered by this

Convention. The members of the Committee shall be elected by States Parties from among their nationals and shall serve in their personal capacity, consideration being given to equitable geographical distribution, as well as to the principal legal system.

(3) The members of the Committee shall be elected by secret ballot from a list of persons nominated by States Parties. Each State Party may nominate one person from among its own nationals.

(4) The initial election to the Committee shall be held no later than six months after the date of the entry into force of the present Convention and thereafter every second year. At least four months before the date of each election, the Secretary-General of the United Nations shall address a letter to States Parties inviting them to submit their nominations within two months. The Secretary-General shall subsequently prepare a list in alphabetic order of all persons thus nominated, indicating State Parties which have nominated them, and shall submit it to the States Parties to the present Convention.

(5) The elections shall be held at meetings of States Parties convened by the Secretary-General at United Nations Headquarters. At those meetings, for which two-thirds of States Parties shall constitute a quorum, the persons elected to the Committee shall be those who obtain the largest number of votes and an absolute majority of the votes of the representatives of States Parties and voting.

(6) The members of the Committee shall be elected for a term of four years. They shall be eligible for re-election, if renominated. The term of five of the members elected at the first election shall expire at the end of two years; immediately after the first election, the names of those five members shall be chosen by lot by the Chairman of the meeting.

(7) If a member of the Committee dies or resigns or declares that for any other cause he or she can no longer perform the duties of the Committee, the State Party which nominated the members shall appoint another expert from among its nationals to serve for the remainder of the term, subject to the approval of the Committee.

(8) The Committee shall establish its own rules of procedure.

(9) The Committee shall elect its officers for a period of two years.

(10) The meetings of the Committee shall normally be held at United Nations Headquarters or at any other convenient place as

determined by the Committee. The Committee shall normally meet annually. The duration of the meetings of the Committee shall be determined and reviewed, if necessary, by a meeting of the States Parties to the present Convention, subject to the approval of the General Assembly.

(11) The Secretary-General of the United Nations shall provide the necessary staff and facilities for the effective performance of the functions of the Committee, under the present convention.

(12) With the approval of the General Assembly, the members of the Committee established under the present Convention shall receive emolument from the United Nations resources on such terms and conditions as the Assembly may decide.

Article 44: (1) States Parties undertakes to submit to the Committee, through the Secretary-General of the United Nations, reports on the measures they have adopted which give effect to the rights recognized herein and on the progress made on the enjoyment of those rights;

(a) within two years of the entry into force of the convention for the State Party concerned;

(b) thereafter every five years.

(2) Reports made under the present Article shall indicate factors and difficulties, if any, affecting the degree of fulfillment of the obligations under the present Convention. Reports shall also contain sufficient information to provide the Committee with a comprehensive understanding of the implementation of the Convention in the country concerned.

(3) A State Party which has submitted a comprehensive initial report to the Committee need not, in its subsequent reports submitted in accordance with paragraph 1 (b) of the present Article, repeat basic information previously provided.

(4) The Committee may request from States Parties further information relevant to the implementation of the Convention.

(5) The Committee shall submit to the General Assembly, through the Economic and Social Council, every two yeas, reports on its activities.

(6) States Parties shall make their reports widely available to the public in their own countries.

Article 45: In order to foster the effective implementation of the Convention and to encourage international co-operation in the field covered by the convention;

(a) The specialized agencies, the United Nations Children's Fund (UNICEF), and other United Nations Organs shall be entitled to be represented at the consideration of the implementation of such provisions of the present Convention as fall within the scope of their mandate. The Committee may invite the specialized agencies, the United Nations Children's Fund and other competent bodies as it may consider appropriate to provide expert advice on the implementation of the Convention in areas falling within the scope of their respective mandates. The Committee may invite the specialized agencies, the United Nations Children's Fund and other United Nations organs to submit reports on the implementation of the Convention on areas falling within the scope of their activities;

(b) The Committee shall transmit, as it may consider appropriate, to the specialized agencies, the United Nations Children's Fund and other competent bodies, any reports from States Parties that contain a request or indicate a need, for technical advice or assistance, along with the Committee's observations and suggestions, if any, on these requests or indications;

(c) The Committee may recommend to the General Assembly to request the Secretary-General to undertake on its behalf studies on specific issues relating to the rights of the child;

(d) The Committee may make suggestions and general recommendations based on information received pursuant to Articles 44 and 45 of the present Convention. Such suggestion and general recommendations shall be transmitted to any State Party concerned and reported to the General Assembly, together with comments, if any, from States Parties.

PART III

Article 46: The present Convention shall be open for signature by all States.

Article 47: The present Convention is subject to ratification. Instruments of ratification shall be deposited with the Secretary-General of the United Nations.

Article 48: The present Convention shall remain open for accession by any state. The instruments of accession shall be deposited with the Secretary-General of the United Nations.

Article 49: (1) The present Convention shall enter into force on the thirtieth day following the date of deposit with the Secretary-General of the United Nations of the twentieth instrument of ratification or accession.

(2) For each State ratifying or acceding to the Convention after the deposit of the twentieth instrument of ratification or accession, the Convention shall enter into force on the thirtieth day after the deposit by such State of its instrument of ratification or accession.

Article 50: (1) Any State Party may propose an amendment and file it with the Secretary-General of the United Nations. The Secretary-General shall thereupon communicate the proposed amendment to States Parties, with a request that they indicate whether they favour a conference of States Parties for the purpose of considering and voting upon the proposals. In the event that, within four months from the date of such communication, at least one-third of the States Parties favour such a conference, the Secretary-General shall convene the conference under the auspices of the United Nations. Any amendment adopted by a majority of States Parties present and voting at the conference shall be submitted to the General Assembly for approval.

(2) An amendment adopted in accordance with Paragraph 1 of the present Article shall enter into force when it has been approved by the General Assembly of the United Nations and accepted by a two-thirds majority of States Parties.

(3) When an amendment enters into force, it shall be binding on those States Parties which have accepted it, other States Parties still being bound by the provisions of the present Convention and any earlier amendments which they have accepted.

Article 51: (1) The Secretary-General of the United Nations shall receive and circulate, to all States the text of reservations made by States at the time of ratification or accession.

(2) A reservation incompatible with the object and purpose of the present Convention shall not be permitted.

(3) Reservations may be withdrawn at any·time by notification to the effect addressed to the Secretary-General of the United Nations, who shall then inform all States. Such notification shall take effect on the date on which it is received by the Secretary-General.

Article 52: A State Party may denounce the present Convention by written notification to the Secretary-General of the United Nations. Denunciation becomes effective one year after the date of receipt of the notification by the Secretary-General.

Article 53: The Secretary-General of the United Nations is designated as the depository of the present convention.

Article 54: The original of the present Convention of which the Arabic, Chinese, English, French, Russian and Spanish texts are equally authentic, shall be deposited with the Secretary-General of the United Nations.

In witness thereof the Undersigned plenipotentiaries, being duly authorized thereto by their respective Governments, have signed the present Convention.